Learn *to* Play *Piano*

IN 24 HOURS

John Dutton

FOREWORD

Hi, and welcome to the Play Piano In 24 Hours. First of all, let's answer the most obvious question – is this for real? Can you actually learn to play the piano in just 24 chapters?

Well, even if you just work your way through the early chapters, then yes, you should certainly learn a lot about playing the piano. Perhaps more than you thought possible. But the more you get into the book, the more you'll get an understanding of what 'learning' is really about. One of the best things about playing a musical instrument – maybe the best – is that you never stop learning. It's something that lasts a lifetime, if you want it to...

That is not to say there is always going to be an easy, straightforward learning curve ahead. Learning a musical instrument is full of highs, and a few lows too! Sometimes you will probably feel that you are just not getting anywhere, but everyone, even the greatest players, has times like that. The trick is to keep going: suddenly you'll be able to do something that once seemed impossible. Once you've tasted that feeling, it's addictive – and you'll want more.

But don't think we're going to cut any corners. Playing an instrument is not just about being able to pull off a few flashy-sounding tricks, it's about being something far greater – a musician. Being aware of what, and as much as possible why, things are happening is just as important as technical prowess. So, right from the start, you're going to see how playing and reading music go hand in hand, and get an understanding of the musical 'nuts & bolts' that come together to make things happen. Everybody learns at a different pace, so don't be afraid to feel comfortable with each chapter before moving on to the next one.

Playing any instrument is all about making music, and that is something that comes from within yourself. Music is all about how it makes you feel, after all. So when you make music, even if you've only just started, remember that you're expressing your own, unique personality. And above all – have fun!

JOHN DUTTON, 2008

© 2010 Omnibus Press
(A Division of Music Sales Ltd)
14-15 Berners Street, London W1T 3LJ, UK.

Exclusive Distributors:
Music Sales Limited
Distribution Centre, Newmarket Road,
Bury St Edmunds, Suffolk IP33 3YB, UK.
Music Sales Corporation
257 Park Avenue South,
New York, NY10010, USA.
Macmillan Distribution Services
56 Parkwest Drive,
Derrimut Vic 3000,
Australia.

Order No. OP53020
ISBN 978-0-7119-4117-5

Project Editor: David Harrison.
Music processed by Paul Ewers.
Cover and book design by Fresh Lemon.
DVD mastered by Technote Media.

Special thanks to City Lit for all their help.

Printed in the EU.

A catalogue record for this book is available from the British Library.

Your Guarantee of Quality
As publishers, we strive to produce every book to the highest commercial standards. The music has been freshly engraved and the book has been carefully designed to minimise awkward page turns and to make playing from it a real pleasure. Particular care has been given to specifying acid-free, neutral-sized paper made from pulps which have not been elemental chlorine bleached. This pulp is from farmed sustainable forests and was produced with special regard for the environment. Throughout, the printing and binding have been planned to ensure a sturdy, attractive publication which should give years of enjoyment. If your copy fails to meet our high standards, please inform us and we will gladly replace it.

www.musicsales.com

CONTENTS `00:00`

INTRODUCTION 1: THE PIANO AS WE KNOW IT TODAY

You may already have chosen or bought your piano but, by way of introduction, we are going to have a quick look at how and why the piano evolved; the different types of piano available; and what makes them all unique.

THE PIANO: HOW IT STARTED

The piano as we know it evolved as a development of the *harpsichord*. Outwardly similar to a small grand piano, the harpsichord was a keyboard instrument that used a broadly similar principle of construction – inside the case was a large soundboard attached to a sturdy, main frame. Across the soundboard a series of strings were tightly stretched. Pressing a note on the harpsichord's keyboard would, via an elaborate mechanical action, trigger a plectrum, which in turn would pluck a string. The resulting sound, amplified through the wooden soundboard, was beautifully sweet and is immediately characteristic of *Baroque* period keyboard music.

However, there was one major flaw with the harpsichord, or indeed any contemporary instrument (such as the *clavichord*) that had a plucked action. Despite the best efforts of the most respected manufacturers, it was simply not possible to vary the dynamic level, louder or quieter, by more than a very small amount. However hard (or soft) a key was played on the keyboard, the note would be heard at virtually the same level of volume.

Some designs tried to enhance the overall sound to compensate for this shortcoming; instead of each key plucking one string, two or three were tried, at higher or lower *pitches*. These were often used in conjunction with *two manual* instruments, which also allowed for greater contrast of tone.

But despite these innovations, the dynamic limitations of the harpsichord were still apparent. As music moved into the *Classical* period and on towards the *Romantic* period, composers were making greater demands of musical instruments – they wanted both more power and excitement in their music, as well as subtlety and delicacy. By the latter part of the 18th century, the harpsichord had started to lose favour to a new instrument, one that could start to provide these characteristics – the piano.

Although the piano had a similar arrangement of soundboard and strings, it was its action (using hammers to strike the strings as opposed to the plucking action of a harpsichord) that allowed for far greater variation of volume and tone. The action also allowed the hammer to return to its original position after a note had been struck, leaving the string to vibrate freely and give the sound more sustain.

Bartolomeo Cristofori, acknowledged as the inventor of the piano, built his first example around the year 1700 although, as mentioned above, it was much later that century before it usurped the harpsichord as the most popular keyboard instrument. By that time several

refinements had been made to his original design and by the end of the 18th century there were several well-established piano manufacturers, including the Austrian *Stein* and German *Ibach* families.

PRESENT DAY

Over the next century the piano continued to evolve at a rapid pace. In response to continuing demands for more power and greater range, designers took advantage of the new availability of industrial metals to make instruments with robust iron frames and higher quality steel piano strings. Longer keyboards increased the range of higher and lower notes available. By the end of the 19th century, piano design had more or less peaked – a modern day piano is mainly superior only in terms of manufacturing techniques.

TYPES OF ACOUSTIC PIANO

A grand piano is the most recognisable descendant of the harpsichord, with its horizontal soundboard and strings and its long, distinctive shape. Sizes vary from three feet to 12 feet long: the largest *concert grands* usually only found in large halls or expensive recording studios. With the lid opened, a large grand piano is a formidably expressive instrument, capable of holding its own against a full orchestra or producing moments of great subtlety. Unfortunately a new concert grand is also formidably expensive, which puts it out of the reach of many. However, a moderately-sized domestic room can accommodate a smaller grand piano, and the power and quality of tone they produce can make the space they consume worth the inconvenience.

Upright pianos are generally more popular as home instruments because of their more compact size. As the name suggests, the soundboard and strings are arranged vertically, which makes them ideal to sit flush against a wall. As it is considerably smaller than a grand piano, the sound and tone have a noticeably different quality, yet a good upright can be every bit as rewarding to play. A new upright piano also costs considerably less than a new grand, though second-hand grand pianos can be very good value as demand is limited due to their size.

Finally, it is unlikely that you would still find a piano with a wooden frame, but if you do, my advice would be not to be tempted. They can have a very sweet tone but are notoriously difficult to keep in tune. Iron frame pianos are far more robust and tolerant of variations in temperature and humidity.

ELECTRIC PIANOS

The description 'electric piano' can be something of a misnomer, as there is a clear distinction to be drawn between a 'home keyboard' and a proper electric piano. It is only in recent years that the playing quality of domestic electric pianos has reached the standard where they can realistically be considered as alternatives to an acoustic. A proper electric piano will have a full length (88-note) keyboard, two pedals situated underneath the middle of the keyboard, and, generally speaking, will have a small selection of piano sounds and just a few others (typically strings, organ and maybe vibraphone). If the piano is heavily loaded with other sounds and features, such as auto accompaniment and rows of buttons, the closer it is getting to a 'home keyboard' and less like a serious playing instrument.

Even though the better electric pianos can play very well, there is still something missing compared to the naturally-produced sound that an acoustic piano makes. The relationship between an acoustic sound, and the connection of playing something that has a delicately crafted mechanical action, is one of the most rewarding things about playing the piano. Playing an electric piano, which will normally have a pair of inbuilt speakers to produce the sound, cannot help but feel a bit sterile in comparison.

So while there is no getting away from the fact that in certain situations there is no alternative to the convenience of an electric piano (it can be carried from room to room, and can be played using headphones), if you have the option of going either the acoustic or electric route, I would at least try out a good upright piano, and experience the difference yourself.

MAINTAINING A PIANO

Acoustic pianos need to be tuned every six months or so. It helps if the room it is in has a reasonably stable atmosphere as wide variations in temperature can affect the tuning and, *in extremis*, excessively expand and contract wooden components. Apart from that, no regular maintenance is required, though over (usually considerable) time the playing action may need to be reconditioned.

INTRODUCTION 2: GETTING GOING

POSTURE

I am going to touch on this briefly before we start the chapters proper, as it's something that is at the very core of your playing. It may even seem unnecessary – after all sitting down is sitting down, isn't it? – but bad posture can not only compromise your ability to improve, it can also, long term, give you other problems.

Get into good habits now and it will be to your very great benefit. So without being overly fussy, here are a few, quick things to take on board:

- Make sure your seat has a flat, firm base and doesn't dip in the middle. The bodyweight should be concentrated on your bottom, with the heels lightly taking a natural amount of weight.

- Sit upright, with your back straight, and place yourself slightly towards the front end of the chair – don't sit right back onto it.

- Ideally, sit at a height that allows your back to remain straight, and your forearms to be at an angle that very slightly points down to the floor. This may mean you have to sit a bit lower than you originally thought. Sitting too high can be bad news over time, as your back will slouch as you reach down to play.

- Above all, be comfortable.

Over time, you won't have to think about these things – get them ingrained now and they should become second nature.

PRACTISING

It is easy to have a negative image of practising – with visions of hours spent slaving away and not being much fun at all. And there's no doubt you will have times when you don't feel like it. However, once you've got started, and you feel even small improvements, your interest goes up dramatically and you start to look forward to it. As I said in the introduction: learning, and practising, can be addictive.

The key to making progress is to do something every day. Your body is trying to do something it hasn't done before, so even if you do a minimal amount, say 20 minutes daily, over time you'll make far more progress than doing an hour a couple of times a week. Also, once you've got into a rhythm with practising every day, you'll enjoy the regularity of it. We'll cover what, and how, to practice at different stages of the book. For now, just try and keep up at least 20 minutes a day – this way you really will move on more quickly.

FINGERING

Throughout the book there will be references to fingering. This is to give you the most comfortable and technically helpful hand positions, using numbers from 1 to 5. 1 refers to the thumb, 5 to the little finger, and 2, 3 and 4 to the ones in between. There is an explanation on the DVD as well, for reference.

GOAL: TO ORIENTATE OURSELVES ON THE PIANO AND LOCATE BASIC RIGHT- AND LEFT-HAND POSITIONS

At first glance, the piano keyboard can look a bit daunting. There are 88 keys on a full length piano – how can anyone possibly get to know what all of them do?

Don't worry, because things aren't anywhere near as complicated as that. Music is based around patterns, and on closer examination, you'll see that the whole keyboard is made up of the same sequence of just 12 black and white notes, repeated across the whole keyboard.

In this first chapter, we are going to orientate ourselves around a note known as *middle C*. Looking at the diagram above, you can see that there is more than one C on the piano, but middle C is found, as its name suggests, in the central area of the keyboard, between the two pedals.

Sit as near to the middle of the keyboard as possible, and referring to the diagram above, put your right hand on the keyboard, with your thumb on middle C; your second finger on D; third finger on E; fourth finger on F and fifth finger on G. Just rest the fingers lightly on the notes, don't try and push the keys down yet. Bend the fingers slightly so that the hand creates a small arch.

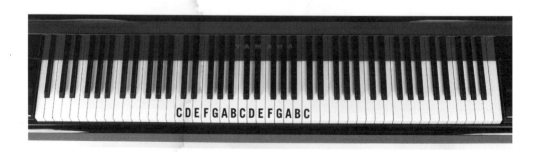

TIP

Your wrist shouldn't be held higher than the forearm, nor dip making it lower than the hand – there should be a gradual line down from your elbow to the hand.

Keep the wrist as relaxed as possible – it's your fingers that have to do the work!

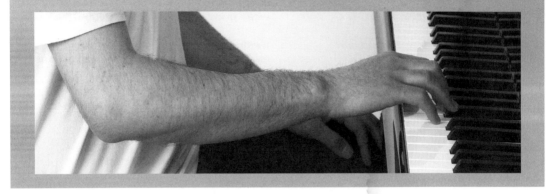

WORKOUT: RIGHT HAND

AUDIO: Workout 1

We're now going to play a simple exercise. Keeping your hand position intact as described above, lift up your thumb slightly and bring it down to sound middle C. When the note has sounded for a few seconds, lift up your second finger slightly and bring it down to play D. As your finger comes down to play the D, bring up the thumb. Follow the same procedure through with your third finger playing E; fourth finger playing F and fifth finger playing G. Finally, play the notes back down in reverse order to reach middle C again.

TIP

The idea is to make the change from one note to the next as smooth as possible – that's why as the next note is played, the previous one is released. Get it right and there shouldn't be a gap between the two notes sounding. Don't allow them to overlap, though – you shouldn't hear both notes sounding at the same time.

WORKOUT: LEFT HAND

AUDIO: Workout 2

You know where middle C is now, so we're going to use that knowledge to help us. Look again at the keyboard diagram opposite, and you can see that eight white notes below middle C is another C. Put the little finger of your left hand on that note, with the other fingers resting on D, E, F and G, similar to what you did with the right hand a moment ago. Then play the notes, C, D, E, F and G, one by one, until your thumb plays G, and play them back down in reverse order to get back to C.

WORKOUT: BOTH HANDS

AUDIO: Workout 3

When you are comfortable playing the exercise with each hand separately, try both hands together.

PERFORMANCE PIECE

AUDIO: Performance Piece

AUDIO: Performance Piece Piano

When you can steadily play the workout with both hands from start to finish, perform it along to the backing track on the DVD.

SUMMARY

Congratulations! You have just learned your first exercise and performed it along to the DVD. While there may not seem that much to it, these early chapters are about being aware of the other things as well - good posture and technique.

Getting really comfortable with these early chapters will reap rich rewards later on. Think of them as foundations, on top of which we're about to start building...

GOAL: *TO BUILD ON THE PREVIOUS EXERCISE AND PLAY A SCALE*

Remember in the previous chapter I said about music being made up of patterns? Well, one of the most important patterns to learn is a scale. Scales (and arpeggios – don't worry, we'll get onto those shortly) really are the nuts & bolts of music. They're not pieces of music in their own right, just technical exercises, but as you move on with your playing you'll appreciate how important they are. At the end of this chapter, you will see how a scale can help us to play a short piece of music.

Let's start again with the right hand in the same position as the previous chapter, with the thumb on middle C. We're going to start playing the exercise from chapter 1, but instead of just playing the five notes up to G, we're

going to play those and then carry on until we get to the next C up the keyboard.

This distance between any note and the next one that shares the same letter name is called an *octave*.

Now there are eight white notes from C to C, but only five fingers to play them. This means some slight jiggery-pokery is called for, but nothing serious – don't worry!

Start the exercise from chapter 1, and play the first three notes: C, D and E. Now, after the third note, E, we're going to change the fingering to allow us to play all the way up to the higher C. Instead of using the fourth finger to play F, as in the previous exercise, I want you to tuck your thumb underneath the arch of the hand and use that to play F instead. It will probably feel a bit awkward at first, but that's natural – most people find it needs a bit of time to get comfortable.

TIP

Your fingers need to do the work here – keep the wrist relaxed and try not to let it turn round to make it easier for the thumb to tuck underneath. Imagine there's something balancing on top of your hand that you don't want to fall off.

WORKOUT 1
AUDIO: Workout 1

OK. So now the thumb is playing F, and you will find that there are now enough fingers left to play G, A, B and C (at the top of the scale). Once you've played the higher C with the little finger, follow the scale back down until your thumb gets to F again. Using the thumb as a pivot, move the hand over slightly and use the third finger on the E. You should now be back to the same hand position that was used at the start of the scale.

Well done, you've played a *C major scale* with the right hand – an important step! It's known as C major because it runs from C, at the start of the scale, to the C an *octave* above. Now for the left hand...

WORKOUT 2
AUDIO: Workout 2

As you may well have guessed, to help us play the eight-note scale with the left hand, we do something very similar to the right. Start with the left-hand exercise from chapter 1, with the little finger on C, and play the five notes up to, and including, G. With your thumb on G, move the third finger over the top of the thumb to the next note, A, and play the last three notes – A, B and C – with third finger, second finger and thumb on the C.

Coming back down, reverse the process and, when you've played A with the third finger, tuck the thumb underneath to play the G. The hand is now back to the position it was in at the start of the scale and you have enough fingers left to play down to C.

TIP

Throughout the book you'll read about keys. A key is just a term describing the seven different notes that appear in a scale. All these notes that you've just played in the scale of C major – C, D, E, F, G, A and B – are therefore in the key of C major.

PERFORMANCE PIECE

AUDIO: Performance Piece 1
AUDIO: Performance Piece 2
AUDIO: Performance Piece Piano
Play the C major scale along to the backing track on the DVD.

Listen to how the two C notes sound similar, yet also how the tone changes between the higher C and the lower C. As part of your practice for this chapter, look at the keyboard diagram again from chapter 1 and find all the C notes on the keyboard. Play them all individually, from the top of the keyboard to the bottom, listening to how the tone changes from high to low, and how they all still share a common sound.

SUMMARY

Work on the C major scale for this chapter, if you're making faster progress than you thought, well done - though don't rush away with things.

It may take a bit of time before you feel completely comfortable with these fingering patterns. However, stick with it, because a lot of other scales, and pieces of music, use them. Later on, when you're doing a flashy run that makes the audience gasp, you'll be grateful you learned your basic major scale pattern.

GOAL: *TO SEE HOW THE MUSIC WE'VE PLAYED LOOKS WHEN IT'S WRITTEN DOWN, AND TO READ, AND PLAY, A SHORT WORKOUT*

READING MUSIC

So far we have been able to orientate ourselves on the piano and play through a basic major scale. The next step is to progress using written music to help us.

We'll take things step by step, so rest assured, it's nowhere near as difficult as you may think. In fact, what it will do is make things clearer in your mind, because you'll have a visual representation of what you're doing.

HOW MUSIC IS WRITTEN: STAVES

Music is written on a *staff* (plural = staves), a template of five lines.

As notes on the piano are played with both hands, piano music has one staff for the right hand and another for the left. The right-hand staff will usually look like this, with a symbol at the start ♭ called the *treble clef*.

The left-hand staff will normally look like this

and have a different symbol at the start 𝄢 known as the *bass clef*.

If you're playing a piece with both hands, the right- and left-hand staves are written joined together, like this:

LOOKING AT NOTES

The easiest way to explain how notes are written down is to see them. Reading from the treble clef, the first note you found on the piano, middle C, looks like this:

...and in the bass clef...

MICHAEL NYMAN
*Nyman is probably best-known for his collaborations with film-maker
Peter Greenaway. Pianist Nyman's work brings threads of Baroque music
together with colourful combinations of vocal and instrumental timbres.*

The schematic below shows you how all the notes on the keyboard are written on the right- or left-hand staves:

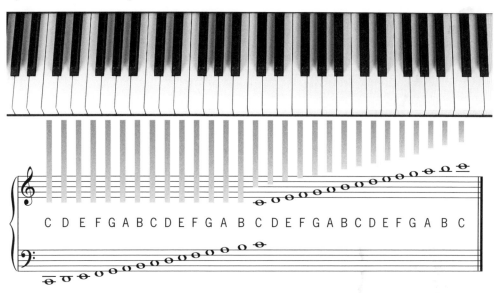

You can see that within the staves, notes are written in either lines or spaces; the higher the note, the further up the staff it is written, and the lower the note, the further down it is written.

SEEING C MAJOR SCALE WRITTEN DOWN: RIGHT HAND

The right-hand scale uses the *treble clef*.

You remember that the right-hand C major scale began on middle C. So let's see how the whole scale looks:

Below each note is a number reminding you of which finger to use.

When a note is higher or lower than the limit of the five-note staff, one or more 'auxiliary' lines are written in, to help you see how much further up or down the note is.

(For instance, middle C sits below the bottom space on the treble clef staff, as that's occupied by D.) These auxiliary lines are known as *ledger lines*. The single ledger line written through middle C is there just to tell you that it's on the next 'line' down.

SEEING C MAJOR SCALE
WRITTEN DOWN: LEFT HAND

The left-hand scale uses the *bass clef*:

This left-hand scale starts on the C eight (white) notes down from middle C. This distance between two notes that share the same letter name is called an *octave* – a term you will come across many times in the book. As with the right hand, there is a fingering reminder below each note.

WORKOUTS

Once you've got used to playing and looking at the C major scale, have a look at the pieces below, which use the first five notes of the scale (C, D, E, F and G), but in a different order. As you play the notes through, they will start to sound like a basic tune.

There is one for the right hand and one for the left.

AUDIO: Workout 1

AUDIO: Workout 2

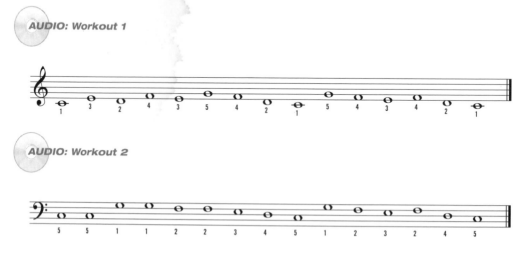

TIP

I've written in fingering, but don't use that to help you find the notes – try and get used to reading the notes on the staves. The position of the notes won't change, but, as we move on, fingering will!

PERFORMANCE PIECE

AUDIO: Performance Piece 1
AUDIO: Performance Piece 2

Play workouts 1 and 2 along to the backing tracks on the DVD. Remember, only do this when you can perform them accurately and at the same speed all the way through.

SUMMARY

Well done! To read and play something is a very important step. To get these basic steps learnt is a massive building block for the future and will help you to make quicker progress later on.

GOAL: *TO LEARN ABOUT BASIC RHYTHM*

We have covered quite a lot of ground already, from posture through to playing scales and reading music. However, one main element has been missing, one that helps makes music come alive – rhythm.

All music has rhythm at its core. Rhythm is based around a pulse, or beat, which can be tapped along in time to the music. Some forms of music – such as dance, reggae, pop and rock – have a rigid beat that often feels natural to move around to. Classically-orientated music may not always have such a clearly defined beat, but there will always be a strong rhythmical base that runs throughout.

AUDIO: Illustration 1

When you listen to music (dance music is a good example) think how you can also feel the rhythm constantly ebbing and flowing, making you nod your head or feel an emphasis every few beats. This is because the pulse, or beat, is structured in *bars*, which are typically two, three or four beats long. The number of beats in a bar makes up its *time signature*.

TIME SIGNATURES

Most pop music has four beats to the bar. This is often known as being 'in four' or in 'four four'. This is a time signature that usually feels comfortable to listen along or move around to. A time signature is always written on the staff at the start of a piece – this is how a time signature of ¼ would appear:

On the staff we need to have a means of illustrating what a beat is, and when – and for how long – it should be played. Let's imagine we wanted to play middle C on each of the four beats in a bar. It would be written down like this:

As you will have guessed, a note written so ♩ lasts for a beat and is known as a *crotchet*.

LONGER NOTES

Longer notes include a *minim*, which lasts for two crotchets. A 4/4 bar of minims appears so:

...and a *semibreve*, which lasts for the whole bar:

SHORTER NOTES

Quavers last for half a crotchet. A quaver written on its own looks like this ♪ When two or more are written in sequence, they are joined together. This is a whole 4/4 bar of quavers (eight of them, as they are half a beat each):

And finally, semiquavers are just a quarter of a beat long. That is four to each beat of the bar, and 16 in a whole bar of 4/4. A single semiquaver is written in a similar way to a single quaver, with a tail ♬ but when there are two or more in a row, they are written joined up. Below is an illustration of a whole bar of semiquavers:

BAR LINES

To separate bars on the staff, a bar line is written in at the end of each bar. This is essential because most music is made up from more than one bar!

In a three-minute pop song, for instance, there would be around 100 bars. At the very end of a piece of music, there are two bold bar lines called a double bar.

WORKOUT

Of course, a bar can be made up from many different combinations of note lengths. We're going to take things step-by-step, though, so coming up are some short pieces, all in ¾ time, for you to get to grips with reading different rhythms. Use the DVD to help you,

and play them as slowly as you need to – there is no rush. Once you're more comfortable with them, try and play them through without speeding up or slowing down too much.

AUDIO: Workout 1

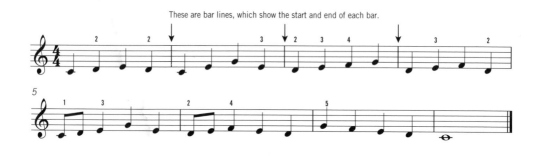

This first exercise mainly uses crotchets, adding in some quavers in the fifth and sixth bar, and a semibreve in the last bar. For these first two exercises you can keep your right hand in the same position, with the thumb

on middle C and the other fingers playing successive notes, just as in the first exercise in chapter 1.

AUDIO: Workout 2

Here's a workout for the left hand, set in the bass clef. Like the first right-hand piece, this first one uses mainly crotchets, with a few quavers in bars 5 and 6, and a semibreve in the final bar. The hand can stay in the

same position throughout – fifth finger on C, thumb on G and D, E and F played with the second, third and fourth fingers.

PERFORMANCE PIECES

There are two performance pieces – both to be played along to backing tracks – one for the right hand and one for the left.

From now on each performance piece will have a guide tempo. For the moment, this will be in the form of a crotchet sign followed by a number – 82 in the case of these first two pieces. This simply means that the guide speed is 82 crotchets, or beats, per minute. The term *bpm* (beats per minute) is a common abbreviation. But I want you to play it at a slower tempo than that, until you're really confident about playing it smoothly and evenly from start to finish. Once you can do that, you can gradually start to take it up in tempo and play it along to the backing track.

PERFORMANCE PIECE 1

AUDIO: *Performance Piece 1*

This first performance piece is a little more advanced, using quavers, crotchets, minims and a semibreve. Use the DVD to help you hear how it should sound.

PERFORMANCE PIECE 2

AUDIO: *Performance Piece 2*

This second performance piece, for the left hand, mixes things up just a little more. Note the four quavers joined together in the first bar.

SUMMARY

Rhythm is all about keeping a steady pulse running through the track. So don't be tempted to rush through the bits you feel more comfortable with. Just build things up gradually and it will all come together.

GOAL: TO LEARN ABOUT TONES AND SEMITONES AND GET ACQUAINTED WITH NEW MAJOR KEYS

There are 12 different notes, black and white, within an octave. Each one of these different notes has its own set of scales and chords. This is nowhere near as complicated as it sounds, because scales are based around patterns. Once you know what these patterns are, you can play them from any note on the keyboard.

To understand how these patterns are made up, we need to explain what *tones* and *semitones* are...

EXPLAINING TONE AND SEMITONES

Tones and Semitones – What Are They?

Let's look at the pattern of C major scale a little more closely. While there are 12 different notes within an octave, C major – like all major (and minor) scales – only uses seven. Therefore, you'll have noticed that not all of the notes are right next to each other. The gap between two notes adjacent to each other (such as E to F, or B to C) is called a *semitone*.

The gap between C to D, or G to A, for example, which have a (black) note in between, is called a *tone*.

All major scales are made up of a set combination of semitone and tone gaps, or *intervals*. Let's look at the interval between each of the notes in a C major scale:

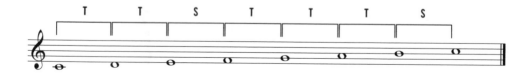

Now, you may have noticed we've not yet encountered any black notes. The C major scale is unique in that it is the only major scale composed purely from white notes. If you start on any other note on the keyboard and follow the major scale pattern of tones and semitones, you will have to play at least one black note, or *accidental*.

Accidentals are known as either *sharps* ♯ or *flats* ♭. The number of sharps or flats in a scale make up its *key signature*.

A sharp sign before a note means it is to be played a semitone higher:
AUDIO: Illustration 1
A flat sign before a note means it is to be played a semitone lower:
AUDIO: Illustration 1b

New Major Keys: G Major and D Major

G MAJOR SCALE

There's an easy way of finding new major keys in order of number of sharps – go to the fifth note of the current scale. As the current scale was C, find the fifth note, which is...G.

G major has one accidental in its key signature. Let's see if you can hear which note in the scale it should be.

With your right hand, start on G and, using the same fingering as C major, play all the white notes up to the next G an octave above. As you play the last two notes, you may sense something isn't sounding the same! Start from G again, using the major scale pattern of tones and semitones to follow the notes up from G – *tone* (G to A) *tone* (A to B) *semitone* (B to C) *tone* (C to D), then *tone* (D to E). The next interval (*tone*) takes us not to F, but to the black note just above it. This note is F♯. The final interval (*semitone*) takes us to the G at the top of the scale.

Remember to keep your hand position as level as possible, and your wrist relaxed. Your fingers have to do the work.

TIP

Remember that the last two notes in a major scale are always a semitone apart. The seventh note will always be the new sharp in all sharp-based major scales.

Here's an illustration of G major scale:

AUDIO: Illustration 2

AUDIO: Illustration 3

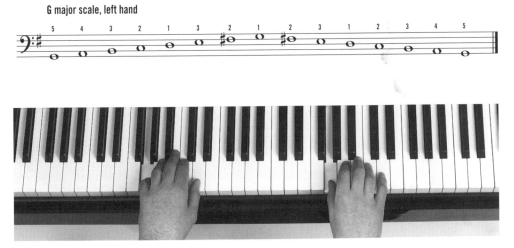

G major scale, right hand

G major scale, left hand

The key signature (in this case F sharp) is normally just written in at the front of the staff. This would normally mean that any F written on the staff would be played as F sharp, but to help remind you, I've also put a sharp symbol in front of the notes.

To find the next major key, go to the fifth note of G major, and we arrive at D.

D MAJOR SCALE

D major has two sharps in its key signature, the F# encountered already, and a new one. There's an easy method of finding out what the new sharp is – the last two notes in a major scale are always a semitone apart, aren't they?

Follow that process through to D major, and you'll see the last two notes are the black note just below D, C# – and D.

So D major's key signature – two sharps – is F# and C#.

AUDIO: Illustration 4

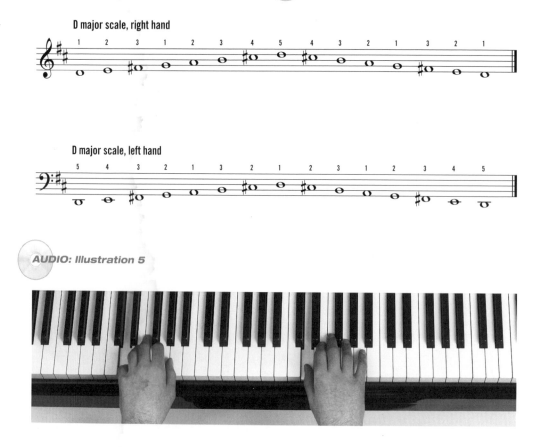

D major scale, right hand

D major scale, left hand

AUDIO: Illustration 5

WORKOUTS

AUDIO: Workout 1

AUDIO: Workout 2

There are two workouts here, in G major and in $\frac{4}{4}$ time. The first one is for the right hand and the second one for the left. Its key signature – F# – is written in at the start of each staff. This means that any F you see on the staff must be played as F#, with no additional sharp sign in front of the note necessary.

PERFORMANCE PIECE

AUDIO: Performance Piece

Here is a short piece to be played with the right hand along to a backing track, this time in D major. Note the two sharps in the key signature – F# and C#. This means that any F or C notes that appear on the staff are automatically sharpened.

SUMMARY

OK. We're about to move onto a big chapter, where we'll start to make music. The early basics we've now covered will be at the core of more advanced chapters, so remember to look back on them from time to time.

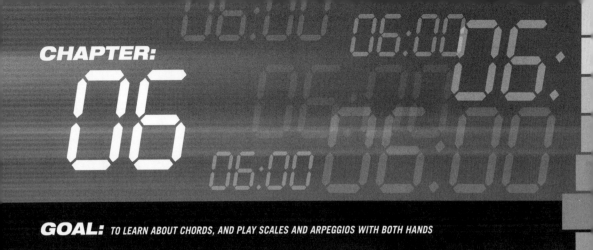
GOAL: TO LEARN ABOUT CHORDS, AND PLAY SCALES AND ARPEGGIOS WITH BOTH HANDS

This is a big chapter, we're starting to bring a few things together that will enable you to start really making music, so stick with it, get these things under your belt and big strides will follow...

PLAYING SCALES WITH BOTH HANDS

The first thing is to play scales with both right and left hands at the same time. You might have tried doing this already, but if you haven't, don't worry, it won't take you

long to get the hang of it. Playing scales with both hands is like riding a bike. Once you have got the hang of it, you won't forget it. It is a pretty essential thing to master, though – so keep at it.

Let's start with C major.
AUDIO: Illustration 4
The thing to get comfortable with is where the thumbs cross over – remember that the right-hand thumb moves first on the way up and the left-hand thumb moves first on the way down.

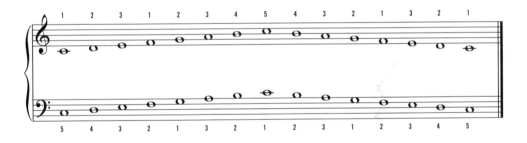

Here is G major – exactly the same fingering.
Note the key signature and remember to play F♯.
AUDIO: Illustration 5

This is written with the key signature (F sharp) at the front of the stave only, so this means any F subsequently appearing in the stave should automatically be played as F sharp.

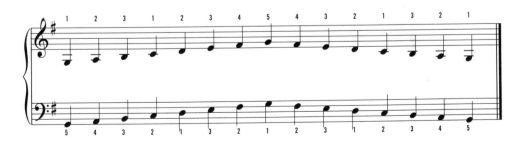

...and D major. Again, exactly the same fingering, and remember the two sharps – F♯ and C♯.
AUDIO: Illustration 6

PLAYING CHORDS
What Are Chords?
Most pieces of music, from pop songs to piano concertos, are made up not only from single notes, but from combinations of notes played at the same time. When two or more notes are played together, they make up a *chord*. As you can guess, the more notes you play at once, the bigger, and fuller, the sound. However, you can't just pick any combination of notes and expect them to sound good – some notes sound good played together, and some definitely don't.

C MAJOR CHORD
The first chord we will learn is C major. Major chords are made up by taking the first, third and fifth notes of the major scale – in this case C, E and G – and playing them together. The notes of a chord are written on top of each other. Here is what a C major chord looks like:

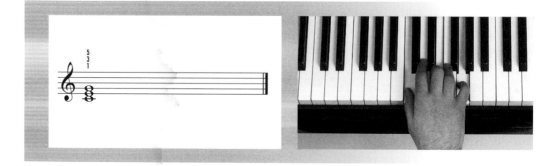

Use your thumb, third and fifth fingers to play the chords, as illustrated above.
AUDIO: Illustration 1

To play a G major chord, just follow through the same process and play the first, third and fifth notes of G major scale together – G, B and D.
AUDIO: Illustration 2

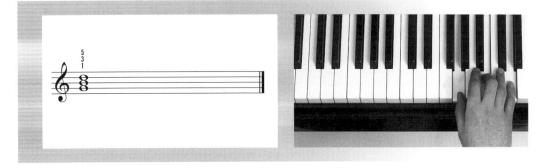

...and D major, using D, F♯ and A:
AUDIO: Illustration 3

These three-note chords are known as triads. As we've only used the right hand to play these chords, let's get the left hand on the case as well...

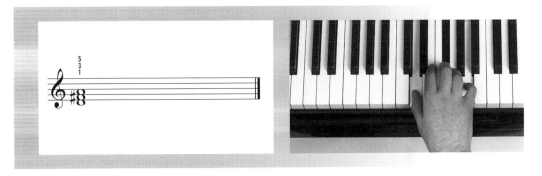

PLAYING CHORDS WITH BOTH HANDS

To play basic two-handed versions of C, G and D major chords, the hands have slightly different roles. The right hand plays a triad, as before, and the left hand just plays the tonic note (C) an octave below, in this first example of C major.
AUDIO: Illustration 7

...and G major...
AUDIO: Illustration 8

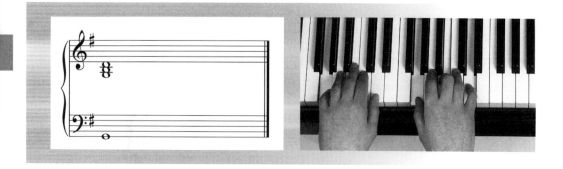

...and D major
AUDIO: Illustration 9

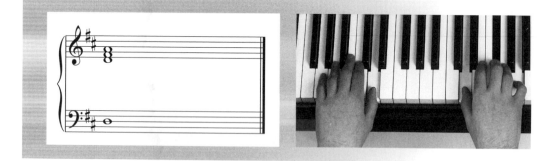

The left hand doesn't play a triad because of the way closely-spaced notes sound when you go further down the keyboard. We'll cover voicings at a later stage of the book, which will expand on this further.

ARPEGGIOS

Arpeggios use the notes of a chord played in sequence, in the same way as a scale. The easiest way to understand it is to see it. Here are the arpeggios of C major, G major and D major:

AUDIO: Illustration 10

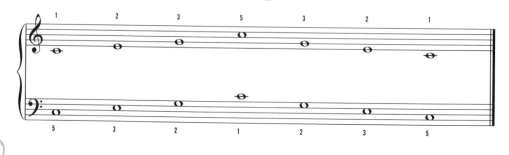

AUDIO: Illustration 11

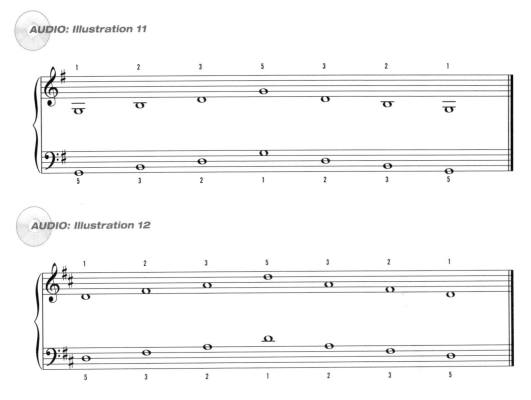

AUDIO: Illustration 12

Arpeggios, just like scales, are really indispensable tools which you will use a lot when playing pieces.

You'll get an idea of this in the workout and performance piece coming up.

WORKOUT
AUDIO: Workout

This workout is the first written for right and left hands together. Don't try doing this first of all – instead work on each hand separately. When you're confident doing this, then try putting them both together.

TIP

Watch the fingering, especially in the fifth bar. It's there to help you, so stick with it even if it feels a bit awkward at first.

The workout overleaf is based around simple scale-based patterns and arpeggios. The fingering moves around a little more than you might expect, so be careful.

PERFORMANCE PIECE

AUDIO: Performance Piece

Similar to workout 1, this uses chords and a slightly more interesting rhythm in the right hand. Again, work on each hand separately first of all and only play along to the backing track when you can play the piece all the way through at the same speed.

SUMMARY

You can begin to see how the basic tools learned in early chapters are used to make music. Playing with both hands is another important step, so well done – and keep at it!

GOAL: TO LEARN ABOUT FLAT-BASED KEYS AND A NEW TIME SIGNATURE – ¾ TIME

FLAT-BASED KEYS

There are two types of accidental – sharps and flats. A sharp sign ♯ before the note means play the note a semitone higher; a flat sign ♭ before the note means play the note a semitone lower.

In the keys of G and D major, the accidentals have been sharps. So where, and why, do we use flats?

EACH NOTE IN THE SCALE HAS TO HAVE A DIFFERENT LETTER NAME

We'll start by looking at the first major key that has flats in its key signature – F major. Starting on F, follow the major scale pattern of tones and semitones, which makes the first three notes F, G and A. The next interval (a semitone) takes us to the black note that sits between A and B. So, A♯, then?

No. While in different situations this note can be known as either A♯ or B♭, the reason why it's known as B♭ in F major's key signature is this:

One of the fundamental rules of music is that each note in the scale has to have a different letter name. You can't have A, as well as A♯ in the same scale. The third note of an F major scale is A, so the fourth note *has* to be a B. Therefore, in the key of F major, that black note is known as B♭, not A♯.

AUDIO: Illustration 1

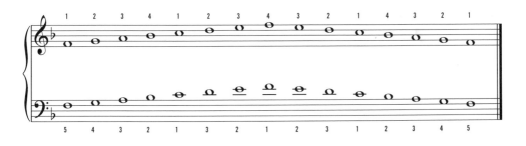

TIP

The right-hand fingering for F major is slightly different to the pattern you've already learnt for C, G and D majors. As before, practise each hand separately before putting them both together.

To find an F major chord we follow the same procedure as before: take the first, third and fifth notes of the major scale – F, A and C – and play them together:

AUDIO: Illustration 2

WORKOUT 1

AUDIO: Workout 1

This short workout is in the key of F major – note the Bb key signature at the start of the staff. There are no chords in this piece, both hands are playing identical single lines an octave apart. Remember that with Bb in the key signature, any B you see written on the staff is automatically played as a Bb.

¾ TIME

So far everything we have played has had four beats to the bar – in 4/4 time. Lots of popular songs and well-known pieces of music are in 4/4 as it is comfortable to feel an emphasis every four beats. There are other commonly used time signatures, though, including 2/4 and 3/4, which simply mean two and three beats to the bar. We are going to look at 3/4 time in this chapter, as it's more recognisably different to 4/4.

It is hard not to recognise 3/4 time once you know what it is – three beats to the bar gives music a very distinctive feel. A good example is the National Anthem. Going from the start, feel how there is a subtle accent every three beats which you can feel running through the whole piece. Try counting '1, 2, 3' along with the music.

3/4 time uses the same rhythmical notation as 4/4. A new feature, seen here for the first time, is the *dotted note*. In musical notation, a dot written straight after a note simply means the length of that note is half as long again. Therefore a dotted minim lasts for three beats, not two, and a dotted crotchet lasts for a beat and a half, not one.

You'll find dotted notes in all time signatures, but they are particularly useful in 3/4 time because it allows odd (as opposed to even) note lengths. A dotted minim lasts for the whole three beats of the bar, for instance.

WORKOUT 2

AUDIO: Workout 2
This eight-bar workout includes a lot of the features normally found in 3/4 time. Notice the dotted minim, as described above, and the minim-to-crotchet rhythm.

We're back in C major for this one. Start with the fingering indicated (right-hand thumb and left-hand little finger) and the hand position can stay the same for this workout – use the same fingering as for the basic exercise in chapter 1. The right and left hands play different notes in places, so be careful.

Note how the dotted minims last a whole bar (three beats long).

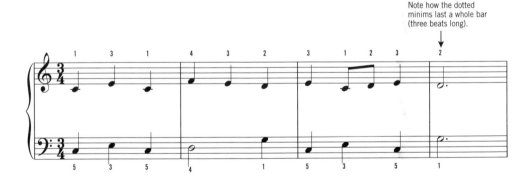

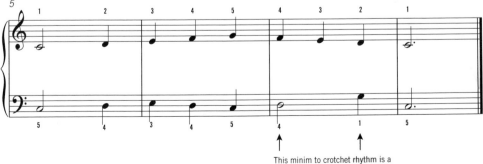

This minim to crotchet rhythm is a common feature of 3/4 time.

PERFORMANCE PIECE

AUDIO: Performance Piece

Let's bring together the things we have looked at in this chapter – the new key of F major and the new time signature of ¾. At 16 bars, this is longer than previous performance pieces, so take your time, work out each hand separately and refer to the DVD for help and playing tips.

Note: Where the hand position stays the same (for instance in bar 2) the music will give you a fingering guide to start with. If no subsequent fingering is given, just use the next fingers in sequence to play the higher or lower notes. So in bar 2, once you've played the first note, C, with the fifth finger, as no other fingering is given for that bar, use the fourth, third and second fingers for the next three notes.

As well as concentrating on the main topics of the chapter – the key of F major and ¾ time – the fingering is a little more involved than before. Where the thumb needs to tuck under in bar 11, remember to keep your hand as level as possible – don't turn the elbow round. The DVD has got plenty of tips for this piece to help you out.

SUMMARY

We will start to explore more flat-based keys very shortly. Every key has a sound of its own – listen to the character of each new key you learn. time will also feature throughout the book. Think of songs or pieces of music you know and see if you can identify if it has three or four beats to the bar.

GOAL: *TO LEARN ABOUT MINOR KEYS AND TO PLAY THEM IN A PERFORMANCE PIECE WITH A NEW TIME SIGNATURE –* $\frac{2}{4}$

MINOR KEYS
There are two basic types of keys in music, major and minor.

The easiest way to demonstrate this is to show you. Let's take a C major chord:

Just as every one of the 12 different notes in an octave has its own set of major chords and scales, it also has its own set of minor chords and scales. The technical difference between major and minor is quite small, but the audible difference is huge – like chalk and cheese.

AUDIO: Illustration 1

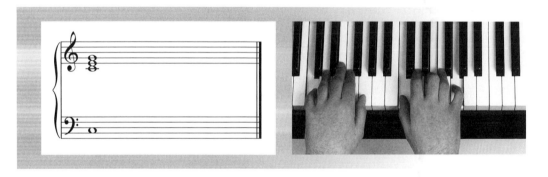

And now a C minor chord:

AUDIO: Illustration 2

As you can see the only difference in the C minor chord is the E♭. In other words the third note of the scale is *flattened* (taken down a semitone). This is a basic rule that works in any key – to go from a major chord to a minor chord, just flatten the third.

In simplistic terms, major chords have a brighter sound, whereas minor chords are darker and sadder. In reality, a lot depends upon the context the chord is used in, as you'll see later on in the book, but you can hear the dramatic difference between the two. And all by just changing one note...

MINOR SCALES

But we're getting ahead of ourselves slightly here. Minor scales are very similar to major ones, but they have a slightly different arrangement of tone and semitone intervals between notes. As you've seen above, you know a minor chord (and scale) has a flattened third, so the opening three intervals will be like this:

Major scale structure:	**Minor scale structure:**
Tone	Tone
Tone	Semitone
Semitone	Tone

What happens during the rest of the scale depends on which version of the minor scale you're playing. Unlike a major scale, which has only one version, there are three different types of minor scale. Don't be concerned, because we start with the pure minor scale, the most easily understood one. Just remember that all minor scales, whatever type they are, have a flattened third.

PURE MINOR SCALES

The first minor scale we learn is A minor. It shares the same key signature as C major, which means no sharps or flats. It also shares the same fingering, so you shouldn't have too much trouble with this one:

AUDIO: Illustration 1

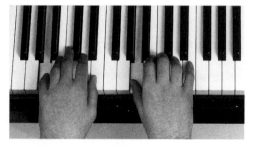

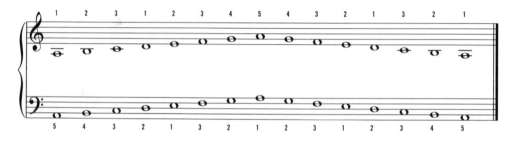

RELATIVE MAJOR AND MINOR KEYS

In the same way that C major shares the same key signature as A minor, every major scale has a relative minor that also shares the same key signature.
So C major is known as the relative major to A minor, and vice versa.

TIP

If you're in a major key and you want to find its relative minor: go to the sixth note of that major scale. For example, the sixth note of C major is A – A minor is therefore the relative minor.

If it is the other way round and you're in a minor key: to find the relative major, go to the third note of that minor scale. So, in A minor, to find the relative major, go to the third note – C. C major is therefore the relative major.

Minor chords are formed using the same principle as major chords. Take the first, third and fifth notes of the scale and play them together – this is the chord of A minor:

AUDIO: Illustration 4

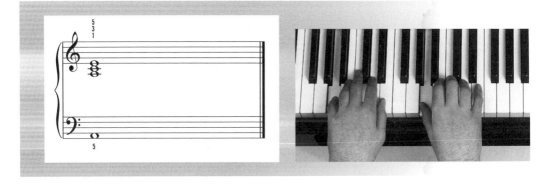

...and the arpeggio...

AUDIO: Illustration 5

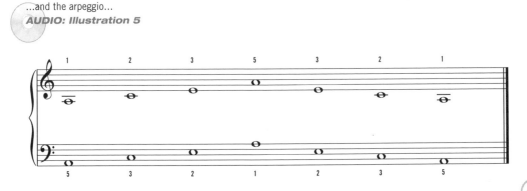

WORKOUT

AUDIO: Workout

This is a basic eight-bar piece structured around A minor. It's in ⁴⁄₄ time and uses a mixture of scale and arpeggio-based notes. You'll notice that both hands are playing the same notes all the way through, an octave apart. When two parts play the same note in sequence like this, it is known as being in unison.

The right hand in bar four is slightly unusual in that the second finger crosses over the thumb. This is to allow the thumb to play the A at the start of the next bar.

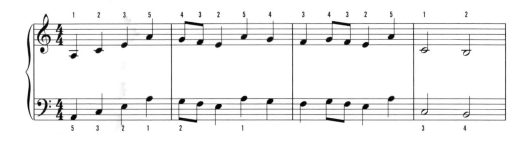

PERFORMANCE PIECE

AUDIO: *Performance Piece*

This is a 16-bar piece using a mixture of single notes, C and G major chords, and A minor chords. Notice how the mood changes depending on the type of chord played. There's one other new feature here – the time signature of $\frac{2}{4}$. This means that there are two crotchet beats to the bar, as opposed to three or four in $\frac{3}{4}$ and $\frac{4}{4}$ time respectively. $\frac{2}{4}$ can sound a lot like $\frac{4}{4}$, but listen carefully and you will feel the music ebbing and flowing every two beats.

GOAL: *TO START IMPROVING DEXTERITY AND PLAYING TECHNIQUE*

TECHNIQUE

We've had a lot to explain to get this far, so well done. Now that we've got a lot of the basic subjects out of the way, we can start to work on really playing the piano.

This next chapter is on technique.

Playing technique is all about the ability of your body to do what the music requires. This can be slow, fast, loud, quiet, or a mixture of everything. Some people's idea of good technique is the ability to play fast passages of music. While it takes skill and practice to do that, there is an awful lot more to technique than being able to rattle off some flashy runs. So while part of this chapter is about improving dexterity, remember that unless you practise slowly and get your form right, improvements will be hard to come by – in fact they may not come at all.

REACHING THE BOTTOM OF EACH NOTE

Back in chapter 1, we learnt the basic importance of good posture and how that relates to your hand position on the piano – keeping your wrist relaxed with the hand creating an arch. I made the point of getting your fingers to do the work.

Now, as we move on and play more advanced pieces of music, we need to start to develop tone, accuracy and dexterity. The first thing we're going to do is develop the feeling of reaching the bottom of each note. It might sound obvious, but consistently doing this, and achieving good tone, takes a bit of time.

To show you what I mean, we're going to use a familiar exercise, the C major scale.

• Put your hands on the keyboard, as normal.

• While keeping your wrist at a normal height, make sure it is relaxed and not holding tension.

• Keeping this feeling, start to play the scale up and down, slowly. You may find that your fingers have to work harder than normal. This is quite normal when you first start to keep a relaxed wrist.

• As you go up and down the scale, try and make sure your fingers reach the bottom of each note. This doesn't mean you have to play louder, think of it as a feeling more than anything else.

• Remember; get the fingers to do the work. It's very important to look at the DVD for this chapter.

Next, I want you to play a C major arpeggio, bearing in mind the same things. As with the scale, play it slowly, getting used to the different feelings.

WORKOUT 1

AUDIO: Workout 1

To help dexterity and evenness of playing, I am going to introduce a way of practising which should have a serious benefit. Listen to the DVD to help you get it right.

Do you remember what a dot after a note does? It lengthens it by half as much again. So whereas a normal crotchet, for instance, is a beat long, a dotted crotchet is a beat and a half long. Looking at this first workout, you can see it is a C major scale made up entirely of dotted crotchets (a beat and a half long) to quavers (half a beat long). While the demo on the DVD will help you hear what this dotted crotchet and quaver rhythm sounds like, a useful trick is to count the bar in quavers – in other words, eight instead of four.

This means play the crotchet for a count of three, and the quaver for a count of one.

WORKOUT 2

AUDIO: Workout 2

Now the important bit – playing in the opposite rhythm. Whereas in workout 1 the dotted crotchet came first, followed by the quaver, this time the quaver is played first and the dotted crotchet second. Using the trick of counting in eight again, play the quaver for a count of one, and then the crotchet for a count of three.

TIP

Don't only play one of these workouts at a time – when you've played one, do the other straight afterwards.

PERFORMANCE PIECE

AUDIO: Performance Piece

This performance piece is a bit more up-tempo – quicker – than in previous chapters. That's your goal in this chapter – which is only after time spent practising it slowly! To get it even, practise the difficult bits slowly in opposite 'dotted' rhythms.

PRACTISING SCHEDULE

It is really going to help if you can put in at least half an hour a day from this point onwards. Once you've got into a rhythm of practising, it isn't that much time really – you may find yourself doing more without thinking about it! Try and break up your practising into sections. Start with scales to warm up, then move onto the topics covered in the chapter, and the performance piece. If you have difficulty with a particular section, just work through it slowly, practising it in opposite rhythms if applicable. Improvements can take time to become evident, but keep your form right, stay with it and you'll get it.

SUMMARY

Playing exercises, and difficult passages of music, in opposite rhythms like this helps even out inconsistencies and improves finger strength. Most importantly, though, take your time and keep a good form, bearing in mind everything we've talked about in this chapter.

10

GOAL: *TO LEARN ABOUT RESTS AND PHRASING*

Imagine you had to read out loud from a book for a couple of minutes. You wouldn't be able to continue without pausing for breath, would you? Music is exactly the same. It needs to ebb and flow, and breathe. There are two principal ways of doing this – the first one is using rests.

RESTS

Music is not one continuous stream of notes. Instead, it's broken up with gaps – sometimes small, lasting for maybe one beat or half a beat; sometimes longer, lasting for several beats, or even several bars. These gaps appear all the time in music and they are known as rests.

Every note length, crotchet, quaver, minim, semibreve and so on, has an equivalent rest. They are written like so:

Semibreve: ○ and ▬
Minim: ♩ and ▬
Crotchet: ♩ and 𝄽
Quaver: ♪ and 𝄾
Semiquaver: ♬ and 𝄿

A bar can be made up from any combination of notes and rests, just notes or just rests. Whenever you see a rest, just leave a gap for however long that particular rest is. You'll soon get to know them.

WORKOUT 1

AUDIO: Workout 1

This workout uses some of the most commonly found rests – quaver, crotchet, minim and semibreve. It's in $\frac{4}{4}$ time – refer to the DVD to help you.

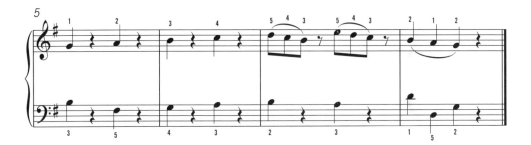

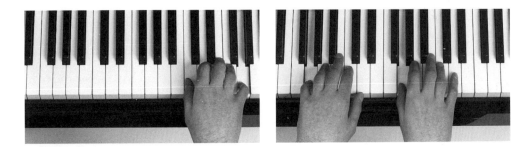

PHRASING

The other way music breathes is through phrasing. Think of phrasing as the length of a musical statement. This can be short, as little as a few beats, a bar, or several bars long. A phrase mark is a curved line drawn over the music on the staff:

Look at the music that lies within a phrase curve and see if you can sense the ebbs and flows within. Where the phrasing curve ends, and another starts, it is a sign to take an almost imperceptible breath – more felt than heard.

Look at this simple four-bar tune, written in the right-hand staff for example's sake. The phrasing curves let you know that the composer wants you to regard it as a pair of two-bar phrases, as opposed to one four-bar phrase. In other words, it needs to breathe after the second bar, where the first phrase curve ends.

AUDIO: Illustration 1

AUDIO: Illustration 2

See also how the phrasing curve has helped to shape the sound of this passage – two short notes, followed by four smooth notes in a separate 'statement'.

WORK FROM THE
SCALE DIRECTORY

When a scale is closely related to others we've just learned, I won't write them out in the chapter. Instead there's a scale and arpeggio directory at the back of the book for new scales; I'll give you a couple to learn in each chapter. The performance piece will be set in one of these keys, so you'll need to go through them.

New Scales From The Scale Directory:
E minor and B minor

The two new scales for this chapter are both minors – E minor and B minor. These are the minor keys relative to G major and D major respectively.

IRVING BERLIN
One of the twentieth century's great songwriters and lyricists, Berlin was renowned for composing almost entirely on the black keys of the piano. Weird, but true, and we wouldn't have White Christmas without it!

WORKOUT 2

AUDIO: Workout 2

This workout set in E minor carries on developing dexterity and finger strength. As before, practise in opposite rhythms to get the passages sounding even.

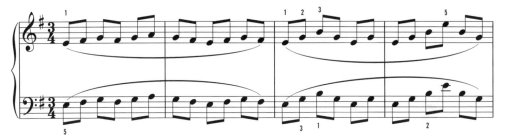

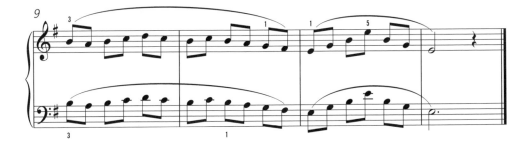

PERFORMANCE PIECE (SOLO)

AUDIO: Performance Piece

From this chapter on, the performance piece is going to be set in a particular musical style. This will be either from a historical or modern musical period.

Where appropriate I'll give a little bit of background to the composer or style.

This first piece is in a *Baroque* style. Baroque music was the prevalent musical style between approximately 1600 and 1750, before the piano had found real popularity. The main keyboard instrument was still the harpsichord, for which the foremost composers of the day such as J.S. Bach and Handel wrote several volumes of music.

One of Bach's best known keyboard works is the series of *two-part inventions* – short pieces with the left and right hands each playing single line (monophonic) parts. Two-part inventions feature *counterpoint*, which is where two or more independent parts are played together, often making reference to or imitating each other. Look at how the left hand imitates the right-hand part when it comes in two bars later. You can find out more about Baroque music in the next chapter.

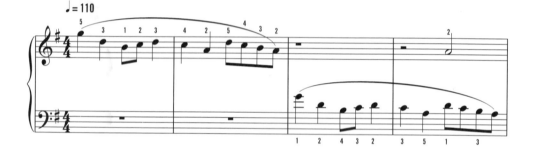

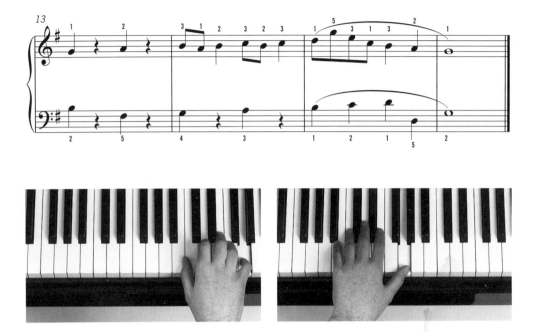

SUMMARY

We're seeing that music is not just a series of notes, and learning about the things that make it come alive. Music is about how it makes someone feel. As a performer, that's down to you!

GOAL: *TO LEARN ABOUT MORE ADVANCED HARMONY AND CHORDS*

NEW SCALES FROM THE SCALE DIRECTORY: A MAJOR AND E MAJOR

Learning more about chords and harmony – the way chords are structured and made up – allows us to put more colour and variation into our music. The first aspect of this to get our attention is inversions.

PARTIAL FIRST AND SECOND INVERSIONS (RIGHT HAND)

Inverted chords use the same notes as root position chords, but swap around the notes so that the tonic, or key note, is no longer at the bottom. Look at this illustration of the C major root position triad and the C major first inversion triad:

AUDIO: Illustration 1

INVERTED CHORDS

Every chord we have learnt and played so far has been in what is called *root position*. This means that the tonic, or key note, is at the bottom of the chord. For instance, look at every C major chord in the book to date and C will be the bottom note.

However, while root positions are important chord structures, play a few in sequence and they sound a bit one-dimensional. Most music is not written purely from root position chords. Instead it uses a mixture of root position and inverted chords.

The first inversion still uses the same notes – C, E and G – but now the E is at the bottom of the chord and the G and C are above it. In a second inversion, the G is at the bottom of the chord and the C and E are above it:

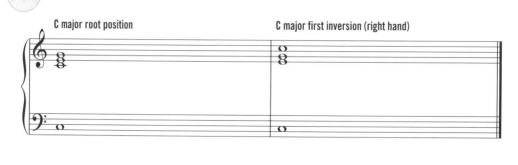

C major root position   C major first inversion (right hand)

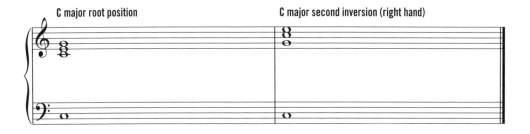

C major root position   C major second inversion (right hand)

AUDIO: Illustration 2

So why do we use inversions? Well, they allow music to move through different keys with smoother changes in harmony. If a composer wanted to move between C and G, using root positions for each chord would sound quite blunt. Going from a C major second inversion to G major root, for instance, the notes can be kept in a similar area and result in a much more subtle change. You can hear the difference by playing the chords in the next illustration.

AUDIO: Illustration 3

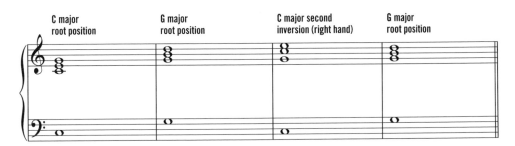

C major root position   G major root position   C major second inversion (right hand)   G major root position

These two chords still move from C to G, but see how the change is more subtle.

INVERSIONS (LEFT HAND)

Inverted chords can be played with the right or left hand, or both. The basic principle is the same.
AUDIO: Illustration 4
However, it is the note that is at the bottom of the chord that determines whether or not the chord is in root position. If both hands are playing a chord, it is what the left hand is doing (the bottom note of the chord) that matters.

Look at the illustrations below:

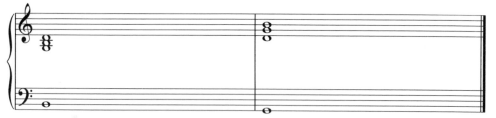

If the right hand was playing on its own, this would be a root position G major chord, as G is at the lowest note in the right hand. However, as the left hand is playing a B beneath, this is G major first inversion.

Similarly, if the right hand was playing on its own here, it would be a G major second inversion. As the left hand is playing a G beneath, this is a root position G major with a second inversion right hand chord.

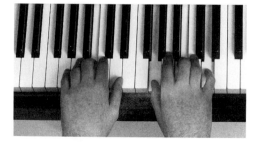

WORKOUT

AUDIO: Workout

Arpeggios can be based around inverted chords as well as root positions. Here's a useful workout that will get your fingers working:

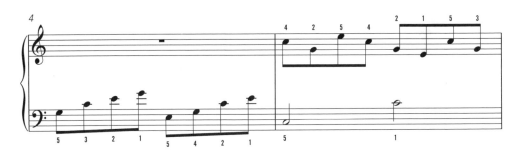

The next part of our chapter covers the use of accidentals and natural signs.

Music doesn't always just use the sharp or flats that are in the key signature.

Even though a piece may mostly be based around a certain key, it can also use notes and chord structures related to other keys as well. So you will often see accidentals written in front of various notes on the staff, telling you to sharpen a note (raise it by a semitone) or flatten a note (lower it by a semitone).

NATURAL SIGN

• When you see a natural sign ♮ written in front of a note, it indicates that the note should be played without accidentals, in its 'natural' form. Look at the illustration below for an example:

This F is played as F sharp, as F sharp is in the key signature

The natural sign used here indicates that this first F should be played unsharpened. Any susbsequent F in the same bar will also be played as a natural

PERFORMANCE PIECE (SOLO)

AUDIO: Performance Piece

This is another piece in a Baroque style. Baroque music is recognisable by its decorative and often delicate style, and use of counterpoint or contrapuntal style – where musical lines interweave and play off against each other. Baroque keyboard music was also written primarily for

harpsichord, but can be played on piano – providing that the more substantial tone of the piano doesn't become overwhelming.

Prominent composers of the period included J.S. Bach, Handel, Vivaldi, Scarlatti and Corelli. There is a list of recommended works at the end of the book, which should give you a good insight into the sound of Baroque music.

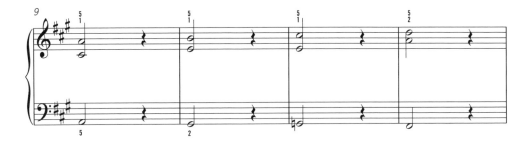

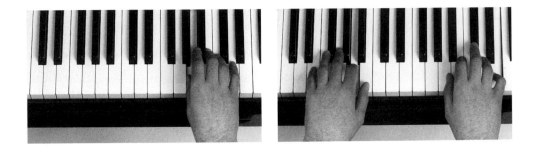

SUMMARY

We are accumulating knowledge at quite a rate here, so look back on previous chapters to help remind you of topics that may not have fully sunk in. Often, things can suddenly click into place, particularly when you come across them while playing pieces.

GOAL: TO LEARN ABOUT DYNAMICS, AND START TO USE THEM

NEW SCALE FROM THE SCALE DIRECTORY: D MINOR

What makes music come alive and reach out to people? It's the human elements, expression and passion. It's time for us to put some of that into practice, and start to make music mean something.

The job of a musician is to inspire the audience. For music to tell a story, it needs light and shade, excitement and sadness, peace and serenity, or all of them.

Once you start to put these human elements into whatever you play, things start to become more than just a series of notes – they become alive.

DYNAMIC MARKINGS

To give the musician an idea of how the music should be performed, a composer will put in dynamic markings, which are written on the staff in the piece. These will be instructions on:

HOW LOUDLY OR QUIETLY TO PLAY

Softly: piano *p*
Quite softly: mezzopiano *mp*
Quite loudly: mezzoforte *mf*
Loudly: forte *f*

TO INCREASE OR DECREASE VOLUME

To get louder: crescendo (cresc) or hairpin symbol

To get quieter: diminuendo (dim) or hairpin symbol

TO GET FASTER OR SLOWER

To get faster: accelerando (accel) accel.
To get slower: rallentando (rall) rall.

ARTICULATION

Another expressive tool is articulation. So far, I've encouraged you to make smooth changes between notes, releasing one as the next one is played. This style of playing is known as *legato*, an Italian term meaning *smoothly*. Now we are going to get to know the opposite of legato – *staccato*.

Put simply, staccato means *detached*. This means play the note as short as possible, to 'detach' it from the next. Notes to be played staccato will have a dot written above or below the note, not after it, so don't get it confused with the rhythmical dotted note.

WORKOUT

AUDIO: Workout

Here is an opportunity for you to get a feel for some of these dynamic markings before playing the performance piece. It takes a bit of practice to increase or decrease volume gradually, so stay with it. When you're playing quietly, remember the technical hints in the last few chapters – keep your wrist relaxed and reach the bottom of each note. This will mean that, with practice, you'll still get a good tone when playing quietly.

Notes on the workout:

The notes in bars 5 and 6 of the workout are marked staccato. Refer to the DVD to hear and see how they should be played.

Where the left hand is playing two-note chords in bars 3 and 4, try to keep the change between them as legato – as smooth – as possible. With practice you should have no trouble doing this with the first three chords. The left hand will have to come off the keyboard between the third and fourth chord.

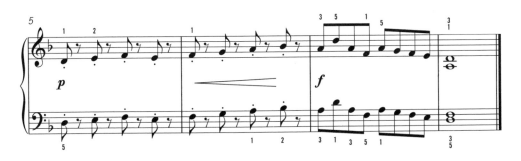

PERFORMANCE PIECE (SOLO)

AUDIO: Performance Piece

This performance piece is based around a different musical style, from the *Classical* period. This followed on from the Baroque period and was generally a less flamboyant, more tuneful style with less use of counterpoint. Several famous composers lived during or came into prominence at this time (approximately 1750–1810) including Mozart, Haydn, Beethoven and Schubert. This was the period in which the piano really became established as the principal keyboard instrument. Some of the greatest and best-known piano works were written during the Classical period, including piano concertos and sonatas by Mozart and Beethoven.

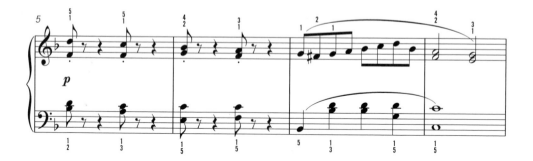

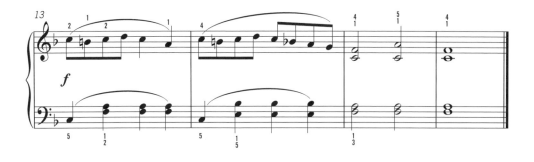

SUMMARY

The use of dynamics will become increasingly important as we go through the book. Dynamic markings can instruct the change to be gradual or instant, so be ready for either.

GOAL: *TO GET POWER AND TONE USING ARM WEIGHT*

New Scales From The Scale Directory:
B♭ major and E♭ major

ARM WEIGHT

Now that we're beginning to play larger chords and put more dynamics into playing, we need to look at the best way to get power and tone while remaining comfortable and in control.

Playing the piano requires effort, but rarely as much as many people think. As with most things, good technique makes things much easier. When playing chords, it's one thing to be able to play loudly (anyone can do that, by hitting the keyboard hard) but it's another to be able to get power and good tone.

The key to doing this is keeping your wrist relaxed, free to move up and down, and using the weight of your arm to produce the power.

Let's try this out. Here's a standard C major chord:

Before you play it, I want you to find and rest your fingers on the notes, without playing them. Then, while keeping the ends of the fingers on the keyboard, pivot the wrist up, enough so the ends of the fingers can feel a small amount of weight.

Then, imagine that your wrist is being very slowly pulled up to the ceiling, by an imaginary piece of string. Keep the wrist completely relaxed, so the hand falls effortlessly down. When the wrist and arm are raised by about three or four inches, combine the movement of allowing the arm and wrist to fall down into their usual positions at the point the fingers hit the keyboard.

The more you allow the weight of the arm to descend, the more power you will produce. Don't worry too much about accuracy at this stage, the priority is to get the right feeling.

- Arm weight isn't just used to help get good tone when playing with power, it also enables you to play quieter chords with more control.

- By keeping the wrist relaxed and varying the amount of arm weight you'll find you can get a fine degree of control over the level of sound. If you also make sure the fingers reach the bottom of each note, you'll be able to play quieter chords with accuracy and good tone.

WORKOUT

AUDIO: Workout

In this workout there is a series of triad chords, played with both hands. The idea is to play each chord with arm weight. Play through the workout at different volume levels, for example try it with power, and then again much more softly. On the DVD there is a visual demonstration of this and I would strongly recommend watching to get the most accurate idea of how to use this technique.

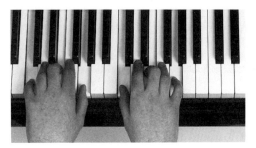

Remember – always get the feeling that you're reaching the bottom of each note.

It is also a useful exercise in identifying accidentals.

*The fingering for the first two bars can be repeated throughout the workout.

PERFORMANCE PIECE (SOLO)

AUDIO: Performance Piece

This piece is written in a Classical style similar to the previous chapter, but with more chords to work on your arm weight technique. The arpeggiated left-hand part that appears in certain places is a common feature in music of this period and is known as an *Alberti bass*. It is a simple but effective accompaniment that allows the left hand to supply the harmony while keeping something happening rhythmically. It is named after the Italian composer Domenico Alberti (c.1710–1740).

As well as the dynamic markings used in previous chapters, a new term, *rallentando*, is used in the last two bars. Rallentando is an instruction to slow down, and is often seen near the end of a piece. A shortened version of the word, 'rall', is a general abbreviation used in all forms of music.

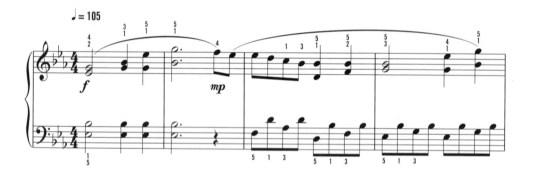

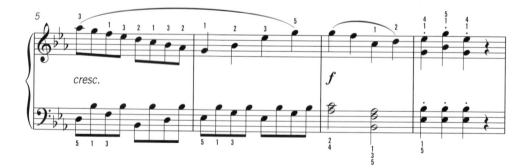

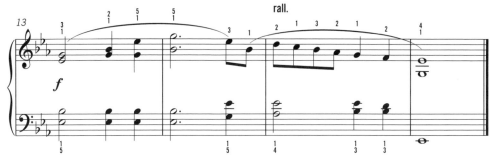

BEN FOLDS

Multi-instrumentalist Folds is best known for his work with the Ben Folds Five, and currently performs regularly as a solo artist and in a number of one-off collaborations

CHAPTER: 14

GOAL: *TO LEARN ABOUT COMPOUND TIME*

NEW SCALES FROM THE SCALE DIRECTORY: G MINOR AND C MINOR

It is time to encounter a new type of time signature – compound time. It sounds a lot more complicated than it actually is; some of the best-known music ever, which you would sing along to instantly, is written in compound time. In fact, once you're aware of the sound and feel of compound time signatures, it's hard to mistake them for anything else.

First things first. Let's look at the two time signatures we have used so far in the book – 4/4 and 3/4, and at what both numbers mean. The upper number refers to how many beats there are in the bar. The lower number refers to the length of the beat. Any time signature with 4 as the lower number has crotchet-length beats.

In other words, 4/4 tells you that there are four beats in the bar, with each beat lasting for a crotchet, and 3/4 that there are three beats in the bar, each beat lasting for a crotchet.

COMPOUND TIME SIGNATURES: 6/8 TIME

6/8 time is probably the most commonly used compound time signature. Looking back on what we just said about 3/4 and 4/4 time, you know that the upper number refers to the number of beats in the bar and the lower number refers to the length of the beat. Whereas any time signature with 4 as the lower number has crotchet-

length beats, any time signature with 8 as the second number has quaver-length beats.

So, 6/8 has six quaver-length beats to the bar. Why not just write six crotchet notes to a bar – 6/4? Is there any point in 6/8? Well, absolutely, yes. The easiest way to explain is to show you. Look at the example below.

AUDIO: Illustration 1

In this bar of 6/8, while you can see that there are six quavers to the bar, they are arranged in two groups of three. This arrangement naturally leads to a feeling of two in the bar, as opposed to six. Play it through yourself, putting a slight emphasis on the first note of each group of three, and you'll start to get a feel for how compound time sounds. Examples of well-known pieces in compound time are *Unchained Melody* and an Irish jig.

OTHER COMPOUND TIME SIGNATURES: $\frac{3}{8}$, $\frac{9}{8}$ AND $\frac{12}{8}$

So the basic foundation of compound time is easy – a bar is made up from quaver-length beats, arranged in groups of three. The most common compound time signatures are:

You can see now how compound time gets its name: a bar can be made up from one, two, three or four groups of three quavers.

NOTATING RHYTHMS IN COMPOUND TIME

You use the same notation in compound time as simple time. However, because the feel of compound time is based around groups of three quavers, you tend to use slightly different patterns and types of notes. Think of the feeling of that Irish jig. The emphasis is on the first of each group of three, so you don't usually have successive crotchets in a bar.

These two bars of $\frac{6}{8}$ show how some of the common rhythms in compound time are arranged.

AUDIO: Illustration 2

See how each group of notes makes up three quaver beats: the crotchet-to-quaver, the group of three quavers, or the dotted crotchet.

WORKOUT

There is a slightly different workout for this chapter. To get into the feel of compound time, we're going to take the two new keys for this chapter – G minor and C minor – and play exercises based around their scales and arpeggios in compound time, using some of the most common rhythms. Remember to keep counting *one*-two-three, *one*-two-three and you won't go far wrong. There is a demonstration on the DVD to help guide you in the right direction.

No 1: this just uses triplets. Give the first one of each group of three a little accent. This will help you get the right sort of feel.

No 2: the crotchet to quaver rhythm is mixed in for this second workout. You'll see this rhythm used a lot in compound time.

No 3: An exercise for both hands, bringing together various notations from the last two workouts.

AUDIO: Workout 1

AUDIO: Workout 2

AUDIO: Workout 3

PERFORMANCE PIECE (SOLO)

AUDIO: *Performance Piece*

This is in the style of a traditional jig. Jigs are set in compound time, which gives them a characteristic rolling gait. Play the first note of each group of three with a slight accent to help this rolling feel. Because jigs are often set in major keys, we're going to start it in B♭ major. After a few bars it will change key (*modulate*) to G minor (the relative minor of B♭ major, remember) but then return to B♭ major at the end.

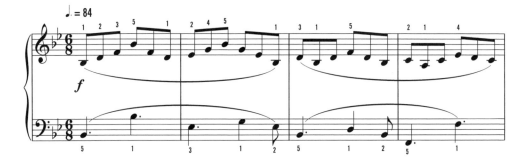

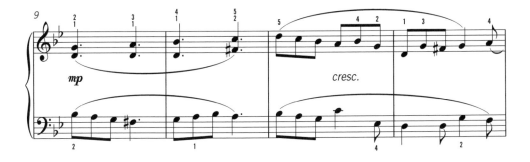

JOHN LENNON and PAUL McCARTNEY
*The Beatles' main songwriters both composed
at the keyboard from time to time: Imagine,
Hey Jude, and Lady Madonna would be unthinkable
without the piano.*

GOAL: TO UNDERSTAND ABOUT AND USE THE SUSTAIN PEDAL

NEW SCALES FROM THE SCALE DIRECTORY: A♭ MAJOR AND D♭ MAJOR

The two pedals at the bottom of the piano case are indispensable tools, although they perform very different functions to each other. We're going to deal here with the one on the right, the sustain pedal.

In short, the sustain pedal is one of the most important things to be able to use, providing it is used properly. It can open up a new world of expression and colour, or make a real mess of the sound. Knowing how to use it, therefore, becomes very important.

Whether you've tried using the pedal or not, here's a simple experiment. Without playing anything on the keyboard just yet, hold the sustain pedal down. Keep it down while your right hand plays a C major arpeggio. Now take your hand off the keyboard, still keeping the pedal down. The sound of all the notes in the arpeggio

should still be sounding, dying away very gradually. Bring the pedal up and the sound will cut off.

So how is the sustain pedal normally used? Well, in two ways:

• As the experiment above shows, it holds on the sound of a chord, sustains it, while you can take your hands off the keyboard. This then leaves them free to get to the position for another chord. That way, as you play the next chord, the sustain pedal is brought up, leaving a smooth transition from one chord to the next.

• When the pedal is held down over a series of notes in the same chord, as in the arpeggio in the experiment, it adds a lot of body and substance to the sound.

So let's put this into practice. Below is a simple chord change from G major to D major (root positions). First, try playing the change without any use of the pedal. Despite your best efforts, there will be an audible gap between the two chords.

AUDIO: Illustration 1

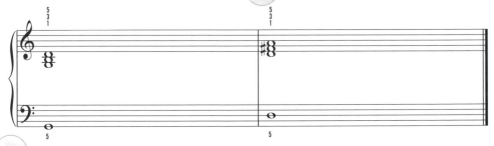

AUDIO: Illustration 1b

Play the first chord again. This time, with your fingers holding down the notes, press down the sustain pedal. You can now lift your fingers off the keyboard and the chord will be held on. Find the notes for the second chord and move your fingers just over them, ready to play. At the same time you play the second chord, bring up the sustain pedal. Do it right, and there will be a seamless change between the two chords.

Timing is crucial here. Release the pedal too early and there will be a gap, too late and the two chords will blur together. Try and play that second chord and bring the pedal up in one simultaneous motion. Once you've got the change between these two chords sounding clean, just go back and forth between the two, re-depressing the pedal to repeat the exercise.

The pedal is also often used over a passage of notes that are based around the same chord. Below is a two-bar passage over which you can hold the sustain pedal:

AUDIO: Illustration 2

As all the notes in the passage are part of the same chord, G major, this sounds fine. Hear what happens when the pedal is held over a passage that moves into other chordal areas:

AUDIO: Illustration 3

It sounds messy, and is a good illustration of how the pedal can be used wrongly. Most of the time, there will be markings on the music to tell you where to use the pedal. These will be horizontal lines written underneath the stave, often with a 'Ped' mark next to it. When the line stops, there will usually be a little vertical line there as well indicating that you should bring the pedal up.

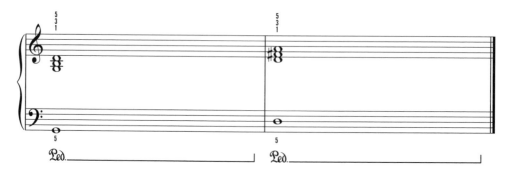

These lines tell you where to start, and stop, using the sustain pedal.

WORKOUT

AUDIO: Workout

We are going to use the arm weight exercise from chapter 13 to help practise the sustain pedal technique. Because there are several chords in a row, it's an ideal exercise to get used to applying, releasing and reapplying the pedal. Take your time, the important thing is to get the feeling right.

As before, the fingering for the first two bars can be repeated throughout the workout. Remember to aim to release the pedal at the same time as the next chord is played, then reapply it to sustain the next chord. As you can see, the 'Ped' sign is not usually used every time the pedal is to be used – just follow the horizontal lines for indication of where to use it.

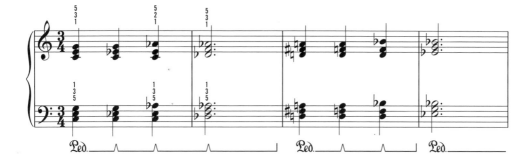

PERFORMANCE PIECE (SOLO)

AUDIO: Performance Piece

This is another piece in a Classical style, with the right hand playing the tune and left hand doing the accompaniment. The dynamic markings lead to a climax at bar 12, but note how quickly the level drops to *p* (piano), where it stays until the end of the piece. In many ways, this piece typifies a lot of the qualities of Classical period music – melodically led, often with fairly simple accompaniment. Use of the sustain pedal is very beneficial here as it helps keep the sound of those right-hand arpeggio phrases ringing

throughout each bar. As the pedalling pattern for the first two bars is repeated for the rest of the piece, a musical term *simile* (meaning similar) has been written in as an instruction to carry on that pattern.

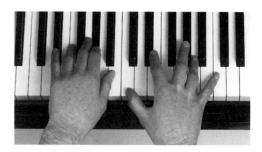

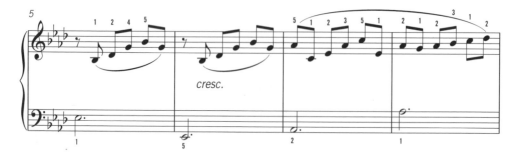

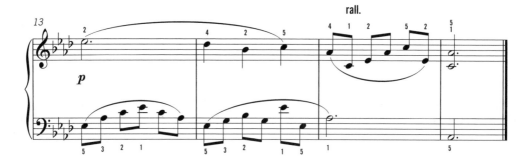

SUMMARY

The sustain pedal may need a bit of practice to use properly, but it becomes ever more useful the further you progress. As we go on you'll see how it can be used in more creative ways, too.

DAVE BRUBECK
Best known for his recording of Paul Desmond's Take Five, classically-trained Brubeck experimented on many tunes with unusual time-signatures.

GOAL: *LEARNING ABOUT INTERVALS AND HOW THEY RELATE TO CHORDS*

NEW SCALES FROM THE SCALE DIRECTORY: F MINOR AND B♭ MINOR

Every chord is made up from a series of intervals. You know what an interval is already – a gap between two notes. An interval can be small, such as a semitone or a tone, or much larger. The most commonly used intervals are contained within an octave.

TIP

Remember that intervals refer to the gap between any two notes, not just from middle C or in the key of C major. I've only used that scale as a reference here.

Within an octave, intervals are described as seconds, thirds, fourths, fifths, sixths and sevenths. These, as you may guess, simply refer to how many notes apart the interval is.

For instance, a second above middle C is D, the second note. A third above middle C is E, the third note. A fourth above middle C is F, the fourth note. And so on, until you reach the C at the top of the octave.

As we go on and explore new territory, it is increasingly important for you to know basic intervals. It helps you understand not only how chords are made up, but how music sounds as a whole, and how it is put together.

BASIC INTERVALS

While an interval is the distance between any two notes, in the same key or not, it will help to refer to a scale, so let's look at C major.

However, as you can see, seconds, thirds, sixths and sevenths have two types of interval – major and minor. Remember, an interval is the distance between any two notes – including all of the black notes. So while C to E is a third, so is C to E♭.

The larger interval, C to E, occurs in the major scale, so it is known as a *major third*.
The slightly smaller interval (by a semitone) of C to E♭ occurs in the minor scale, so it is known as a *minor third*.

Major Third

Minor Third

The same process applies to the other major and minor intervals – seconds, sixths and sevenths. Major and minor intervals are always a semitone apart, with the major interval the larger.

You can work out intervals mathematically, by counting the semitones between each one:

Minor 2nd: semitone
Major 2nd: 2 semitones
Minor 3rd: 3 semitones
Major 3rd: 4 semitones
Perfect 4th: 5 semitones
Perfect 5th: 7 semitones
Minor 6th: 8 semitones
Major 6th: 9 semitones
Minor 7th: 10 semitones
Major 7th: 11 semitones
Octave: 12 semitones

While using this method can be useful to work out intervals from a written part, when playing or listening to music, it is much better to try and get used to the sound of different intervals. Every time you learn a new scale, notice what the interval is between different notes of the scale. This will help you see how they are then used in chords.

HOW THESE RELATE TO CHORDS

Look back at some of the root position and inverted chords you know already and listen to how they are made up from intervals. A C major root position triad, for instance, is made up from a major third (C to E) with a minor third on top (E to G).

A C major first inversion triad is made up from a minor third (E to G) and a perfect fourth (G to C).

WORKOUT 1

AUDIO: Workout 1

Here is an exercise using all the intervals that we have talked about above, using D for a reference note.

WORKOUT 2

AUDIO: Workout 2

This time, the notes are arranged in a less structured order. Try and identify the intervals that occur between each note.

PERFORMANCE PIECE (SOLO)

AUDIO: Performance Piece

We are going to move on very slightly to a late Classical period piece for this chapter, in the style of Beethoven. Beethoven was one of the very most significant, and remarkable, composers. He wrote some of his finest works despite the gradual loss of his hearing, and his music bridged the simplicity of the Classical period with the more dynamic and powerful sound of the Romantic period. His lifespan (1770–1827) coincided with

massive political and industrial change, the turbulence of which can be heard in his music. So what does this mean in terms of performance? Well, being in the style of an earlier Beethoven work, it still has many of the characteristics of the Classical period – melodically led, with a relatively straightforward accompaniment. There is a glimpse of the aggression that appears more commonly in his later works, but it is restrained to remain in keeping with the Classical genre. The left hand plays two-note octave chords in this piece, which may be a bit of a stretch for some. The workouts in this chapter both feature successive notes an octave apart, which will help to develop your stretch.

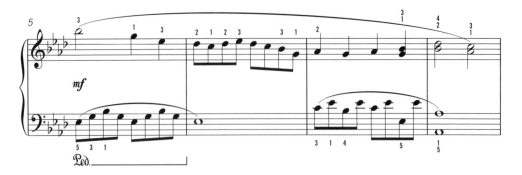

SUMMARY

We are stepping up a gear in this chapter, with more demanding workouts and performance pieces. As always, slow practice is the key to making it happen. Keep your intervals knowledge up by looking at chords and identifying the intervals between each individual note.

GOAL: *TO INTRODUCE MORE DYNAMICS AND RHYTHM*

NEW SCALES FROM THE SCALE DIRECTORY: B MAJOR AND F♯ MINOR

In this final third of the book, we're going to continue to develop knowledge of more advanced piano music, crossing over into more advanced and different types of music. We'll also further develop technique to help us play these more demanding pieces, which for now carry on in the *Romantic* style...

Romantic Period (approximately 1800–1900)
As the style of music moved out of the Classical and onto the Romantic period, music became more demanding to play. The turbulent events of the late 18th and early 19th centuries – revolutions, civil wars

and vast political change – were all reflected in the music of the time. Music became more dynamic, going to the extremes of power and emotion.

The piano really came of age in the Romantic period and matured into the formidably powerful and expressive instrument it is today. As I explained in the previous chapter, Beethoven was one of the composers who helped develop the Romantic style, and we're going to base this chapter around another example of his style of music.

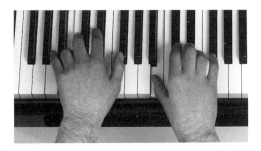

WORKOUT 1

AUDIO: Workout 1
Dexterity Exercise based around B major

WORKOUT 2

AUDIO: *Workout 2*
Dexterity exercise based around F# minor

These two workouts feature a lot of semiquavers, which
may look a bit daunting, but don't let them throw you.
You can play them as slowly as you like, and only bring
them up to a speed that you feel comfortable with.

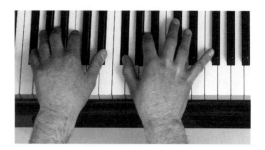

PERFORMANCE PIECE (SOLO)

Beethoven wrote a series of short pieces for piano called *sonatinas*, in which style this performance piece is written. Unlike *sonatas*, which were often lengthy works written in three or four separate *movements*, sonatinas were shorter pieces usually composed of one or two movements. They are ideal as an introduction to Beethoven's more advanced works.

The first things you may notice in this piece are:

• The time signature of $\frac{2}{4}$ – two crotchet beats to the bar. It is sometimes hard to hear the difference between $\frac{2}{4}$ and $\frac{4}{4}$, but two beats to the bar give an urgent feel, like a march.

• The use of semiquavers. These are half the length of quavers, so there are four semiquavers in a crotchet-length beat.

• A pair of double bars with two dots on each stave. These appear at the start of the piece and again at the end of bar 15. These are a pair of *repeat bars*. Whenever you see these bars (and they will always come in pairs, though they may be many bars apart) you should repeat the section of music that lies within them.

• A new dynamic marking – ***ff*** or fortissimo. This is the loudest marking generally used, though ***fff*** is not unknown!

HINTS AND TIPS

As befits the Romantic period style, this is a more dynamic piece than any of the others in the book so far. Let's go through the piece bit by bit and look at the techniques needed to make the most of it.

• The three chords at the start make a bold statement. Use your arm weight to get these opening chords sounding strong, sweet and confident. The first two are staccato, so keep the wrist relaxed and snappy.

• In the right-hand part in bars 3,4, 7 and 14, there are sequences of two-note intervals which you may find difficult to play initially. There are some notes which would clash if the sustain pedal was used, so follow the fingering and try to keep these intervals as smooth as possible.

• The final tip is to make it as exciting as possible. Use the dynamic markings to steer you in the right direction; make the loud bits loud, the quiet bits quiet, and feel how exciting music sounds when it is gradually brought up and down in level.

AUDIO: *Performance Piece*

SUMMARY

You have taken another big step in this chapter, developing more power and more dexterity. With more advanced pieces like this, you may find that you enjoy working on them, then coming back to them over a period of time. This way you can use new techniques learnt in following chapters. Never consider a piece of music is ever totally 'learnt' – you never stop improving and getting better!

ANNA GOURARI
*Russian concert pianist Gourari's performances have earned her a reputation as a perfectionist, and a starring role in Werner Herzog's 2001 film **Invincible**.*

GOAL: TO INCREASE STRETCH AND DEXTERITY, AND PLAY MORE ADVANCED ROMANTIC PERIOD MUSIC

NEW SCALES FROM THE SCALE DIRECTORY: G♯ MINOR

As the Romantic period gained pace in the early part of the 19th century, performers had to develop their technique in order to play the more demanding music that was being written. The range of the piano keyboard expanded, with higher and lower notes, and chords became bigger, with more adventurous harmony. By the middle of the 19th century, two of the greatest pianist/composers had ushered in a new era of pianistic technique – *Frédéric Chopin* and *Franz Lizst*.

Franz Liszt (1881–1886) was one of the greatest pianists ever known. Many would say the greatest: he was the first performer to play entirely from memory and he enjoyed a high profile as a touring maestro, with a particularly strong female fanbase!

His piano compositions are largely for the virtuoso, and many are still considered to be among the most technically demanding ever written. As a composer, his influence was far reaching; he invented the symphonic poem, a single-movement form of music that stepped out of the more formal approach of Classical period music, and he was a great champion of up-and-coming composers such as Wagner and Debussy.

Frédéric Chopin may have had a tragically short life (1810–1849) but his legacy as a piano innovator is virtually unparalleled. He often wrote very adventurous chords and harmonies, sometimes sounding *dissonant* to new audiences. Yet one of Chopin's gifts was that while his music can be extremely demanding to play, he had a great ear for writing tunes. A lot of his music, mainly written for piano, is strongly influenced by his partially Polish nationality. You can feel the strong nationalistic pride flowing through his works.

Both of these iconic figures played a crucial part in pushing the boundaries of piano music forward. While many of their compositions are for the more advanced player, we are going to base this performance piece around some of the more straightforward characteristics that their music contained. Before we do, we need to get in training, using the following workouts:

WORKOUTS

Romantic period piano music makes a few technical demands. Chords are bigger and need more power, so we need to work on the stretch of the hand. Here are two workouts to help you reach these goals.

WORKOUT 1

AUDIO: Workout 1

A good way to get used to playing bigger chords is to practise them as arpeggio-type – or broken – chords. This first workout will help your hand stretch and finger strength.

Even though the sustain pedal is used throughout the workout, still try to make the join between each note as legato as possible. Though you'll sometimes find it necessary to jump a bit from one note to the next, try and keep a good form as much as you can.

This workout shows you how the sustain pedal can be used more creatively. Hear how big the chords sound as the pedal is held on for two bars at a time.

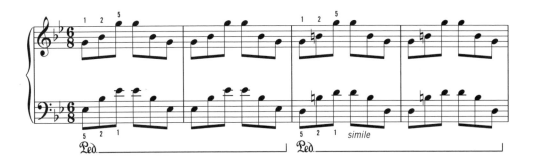

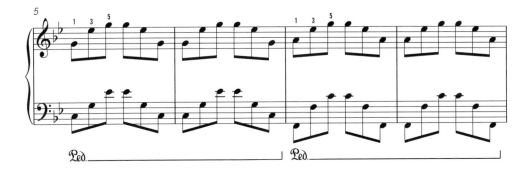

WORKOUT 2

AUDIO: Workout 2

This is an out-and-out dexterity exercise, in the style of one of Lizst's celebrated pupils, Carl Czerny. Czerny wrote many series of exercises for the piano that are useful tools for developing technique. As before, practise slowly and in opposite rhythms to get it sounding even. It is essentially scale-based, so it lies underneath the hand pretty well.

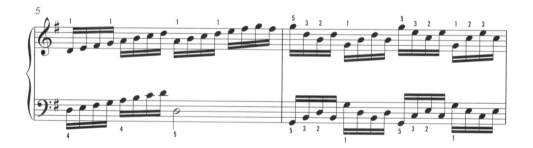

PERFORMANCE PIECE (SOLO)

AUDIO: Performance Piece

This is a tuneful piece in the style of a Chopin nocturne – a name often given to a Romantic period piece with a right-hand melody and broken (i.e. arpeggiated) left-hand accompaniment. The § time signature helps give the left hand a flowing, rolling feel, above which the right hand plays the melody.

A new dynamic marking appears – the accent symbol > seen firstly on the opening chord of the first and second bars. This is an instruction to play the note or chord with a firm accent. Use arm weight to make the chord powerful, but not harsh.

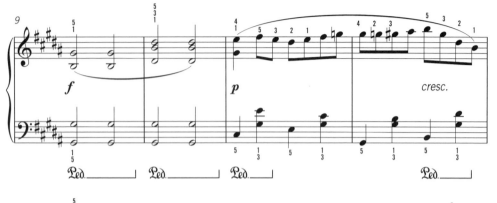

TIP

There are a few hints and tips on playing this piece:

- The dynamic levels can change either gradually or quite abruptly. Remember that gradual changes in volume can be either marked as hairpin symbols or *cresc* and *dim*.

- Where the left hand has to jump from lower to higher chords and notes, practise this hand on its own and keep it slow until you're really accurate.

- The third intervals played in a row in bars 1 and 2 are not as hard as you might think. Try to keep them as legato as possible.

- The pedalling is a bit snappier than in previous pieces. Notice how it's often held down for just a couple of beats so it doesn't clash with the next part of the bar.

GOAL: TO LEARN AND PLAY THE ADVANCED CHORDS AND HARMONY THAT MAKE UP THE COLOURS OF IMPRESSIONIST MUSIC

We're going to learn about some of the most beautiful and interesting music of the Romantic period in this chapter – that of the French Impressionists.

NEW SCALES FROM THE SCALE DIRECTORY: F♯ MAJOR

Music creates many moods and feelings in the mind. Sometimes just a title is enough to help create an image of a piece of music, at others the music itself can be written to suggest, or evoke a mood or picture.

Some of the most evocative music was written by two French composers – *Debussy* and *Ravel*. Both were important figures in the *Impressionist* movement of music, which in turn evolved with the Impressionist movement in art. Debussy and Ravel wrote many of their works to evoke certain images, such as Debussy's *The Sunken Cathedral* and *Prélude à l'après-midi d'un faune*.

To do this they took influences from many other Romantic period composers such as Chopin and Wagner and added new ideas of their own. In Debussy's case particularly, his dislike of writing music in structured forms let the concepts of sound and image drive his music.

MAJOR SEVENTH AND MINOR SEVENTH CHORDS

One of the cornerstones of Debussy's style was his use of adventurous harmony.

You will have found that some notes on the keyboard clash when played together; they sound *dissonant*. When these dissonant notes are put together as part of a normal major or minor chord they lose part of their opposing qualities and create interesting and challenging new sounds.

At the heart of some of Debussy's harmony is the use of major seventh and minor seventh chords. Both these chords use conventional major or minor triads as their base. Let's look at the major seventh chord first.

MAJOR SEVENTH CHORD

The first chord in this illustration is a straight C major triad. To make it into a major seventh chord, just add the seventh note of the major scale – B. As the illustration below shows, when just the bottom note C and the B are played together as a major seventh interval, they sound quite dissonant. Yet when they form part of the major seventh chord, the mixture of sweet and clashing notes creates an interesting sound.

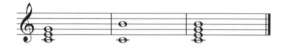

MINOR SEVENTH CHORD

A minor seventh chord is formed using the same principle as a major seventh. Take a basic root position triad (minor in this case) and this time put the seventh note of the pure minor scale on top. This mixture of standard and dissonant harmony had far-reaching influences – it inspired other composers to use evermore adventurous harmony in their music, and it is an integral part of jazz and blues.

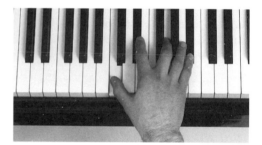

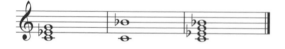

TIED NOTES

One new feature of this chapter is the use of *tied notes*. A tie is a line drawn in directly over the top of two notes of identical pitch, like this:

When a tie is drawn over two notes it instructs that they should be joined and played as a single note – for the combined length of the two notes. There are a few different reasons for using tied notes:

• To get over the obstacle of a bar line, as in the illustration above.

• In compound time signatures such as $\frac{6}{8}$, if a note is to last for the whole bar it is usual to write it as two dotted crotchets, tied together. This helps to keep the division of the bar into two groups of three quavers.

• To make up a note value that is not possible with a single note, for instance a minim tied to a quaver lasts for two and a half beats.

WORKOUT 1

AUDIO: Workout 1

A series of major seventh arpeggios to get your fingers used to playing the chords. You can use the fingering from the first bar for the rest of the workout. Play each bar twice before moving on to the next and when you get to the end, play the exercise in reverse to get back to the start.

WORKOUT 2

AUDIO: Workout 2

This time, a series of minor seventh arpeggios. Again, play each bar twice and reverse the exercise to get back down again. Both of these workouts and the performance piece coming up feature a few high leger lines in the left hand, so refer back to the keyboard diagrams if you need to.

PERFORMANCE PIECE (SOLO)

This piece relies on a lot of expression and subtlety. The DVD gives you a lot of hints and tips, so look at it carefully and listen to the demonstration to help you.

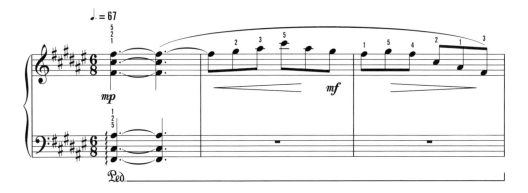

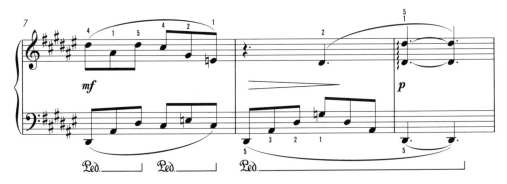

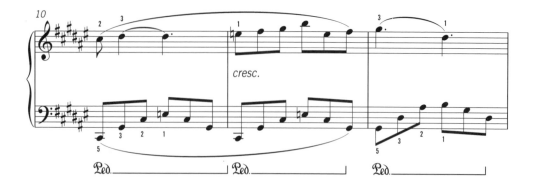

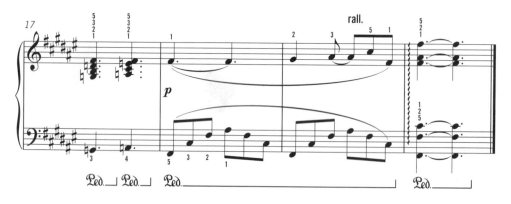

GOAL: TO LEARN ABOUT ATONAL HARMONIES, AND MORE ADVANCED, SYNCOPATED RHYTHMS

NEW SCALES FROM THE SCALE DIRECTORY: CHROMATIC SCALE

Exactly when the Romantic period 'ended' is open to debate. Present-day music such as film scores and soundtracks features the dynamic highs and lows that feature strongly in Romantic music. Many great composers continued to write in a romantic style well into the 20th century – Rachmaninoff and the English composers Elgar and Vaughan Williams being among them.

But during the early 1900s a strong anti-Romantic element gained pace. Out went the accent on emotion and grand orchestration, and in came more forceful rhythms and stark harmonies. The foundations for 20th century music were born out of this movement. To play something in a 20th century style we need to expand our knowledge of harmony and rhythm, so read on…

ATONAL HARMONY

When we discussed Impressionist music, we saw how dissonant harmony – using 'clashing' intervals such as seconds and sevenths – can be mixed in with sweeter harmonies. Well, the philosophy of 20th century music was virtually to throw that out altogether and just concentrate on the dissonant harmonies. This means a lot of 20th century music is challenging to listen to. Give it a chance, though, because in time you will adjust to hearing these unconventional harmonies and the more music you take in, and play, the more rounded a player you will be as a result.

SYNCOPATED RHYTHMS

Virtually all music uses what is known as *syncopation* – accented notes that are 'off the beat'. However, 20th century music makes it more of a feature, which is ideal for illustration.

WORKOUTS 1 AND 2

These short workouts give you a chance to hone your skills on syncopation and get used to some atonal harmony. With syncopated rhythms, break down whatever the time signature is into the value of the shortest note in the bar. In this first workout, the time signature is $\frac{4}{4}$ and the syncopated notes are all quavers. As there are eight quavers to the bar, count the bar in quavers – in eight instead of in four. You'll soon get a feel for how the syncopated rhythms fit in.

AUDIO: Workout 1

AUDIO: Workout 2

PERFORMANCE PIECE (SOLO)

AUDIO: Performance Piece

By previous standards, there is some unconventional notation and fingering here. The overall feel is also a bit stark, with spiky harmonies and aggressive rhythms. In terms of actually playing the piece, there's nothing especially difficult, it's just a bit unusual.

- The dynamics change very quickly. Try to get as big a contrast as possible between louds and softs.

- There is a fair bit of syncopation, specifically on the chords in bars 1, 2, 6, 8, 14 and 15. The easiest way to get this right is to break the bar down and count it in eight.

- There's no use of the sustain pedal because of the constantly changing harmony, so try to make each hand as legato as possible.

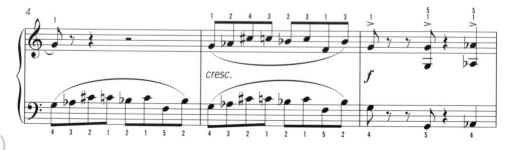

ATONAL HARMONIES AND SYNCOPATED RHYTHMS

CHROMATIC SCALE

Instead of using only seven different notes, as a major or minor scale does, a chromatic scale uses every single note that lies within an octave. This simply means that a chromatic scale is a run of adjacent notes. A general term often used in music is a 'chromatic' run where there is a sequence of adjacent notes.

SUMMARY

While this style of music may sound unusual, persevere with it. In time your opinion of it may change. A lot of the techniques learnt here, such as syncopation and unusual chord shapes, will make previous pieces easier to play, and also put you on a strong footing to move onto more advanced music.

GOAL: TO LEARN SOME BASIC BLUES PIANO AND PLAY A 12-BAR PERFORMANCE PIECE

NEW SCALES FROM THE SCALE DIRECTORY: BLUES SCALE IN C

At the cornerstone of most modern pop and jazz music is blues. In its most basic form, blues is a satisfying and fun to play form of music. After learning about the most important elements that make blues sound how it does, you'll see how these can be developed to progress into pop and jazz.

WHERE BLUES CAME FROM

While slaves in the American plantations worked, they sang songs to help them get through the gruelling conditions. A single member of the work party would start a song, which the others would know and sing a response to. Hence the musical term 'call and response'.

As a result of these origins, early blues compositions were passed from person to person, not written down. So when *W.C. Handy*, an accomplished black musician from Alabama, composed and published two iconic works, *Memphis Blues* and *St Louis Blues*, it helped bring the blues to a much wider audience. In the years that followed, many important figures helped to develop the blues style, such as *Robert Johnson* and *Muddy Waters*, to name but two. *Johnnie Johnson*, piano player for *Chuck Berry*, was a great blues piano player and a very influential figure.

Courtesy LFI

RAY CHARLES
An American icon who shaped Rhythm and Blues, his music was always steeped in the gospel and blues of the Deep South.

WHAT MAKES UP THE BLUES?

You may have heard the expression the 'blue note'. This brings us back to something we talked about in chapter 19 – the mixture of sweet (or 'standard') and dissonant harmony. We saw that in illustrations of the major and minor seventh scales, blues uses a similar approach, using a chord that is at its very heart – the *flattened seventh*. Here is a right-handed C seventh chord:

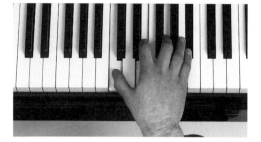

AUDIO: Illustration 1

A flattened seventh chord (C seventh here for example) is similar in structure to a major seventh chord, with one exception. It uses a major triad as its base but puts a flattened seventh on top. This single feature creates an entirely different sound. The interval from the major third (E in this instance) to the top note of the chord (B flat) is what gives the flattened seventh chord its unique sound. This interval is three tones, also known as the *tritone*, and is exactly half an octave. The tritone is an extremely dissonant interval and imbues the chord with an unmistakable character.

Seventh chords can be played in root position or inverted, in exactly the same way as normal majors or minors. Here is how the right-hand C seventh chord looks and sounds when inverted:

AUDIO: Illustration 2

| Root position | 1st inversion | 2nd inversion | 3rd inversion |

Because there are four notes in a root position seventh chord, there are three possible inversions, instead of the two in major and minor chords.

WORKOUTS:

Accompanying A 12-bar Pattern In C

A standard blues pattern, also used in rock and roll, and pop music, is a *12 bar*. It simply uses three seventh chords, played in a certain sequence for a duration of 12 bars. You may well recognise the sound of a 12 bar and it is a good basis for getting into the blues.
Let's have a look at how a 12-bar blues in C is made up:

WORKOUT 1

The three chords in a 12 bar are the tonic (C in this instance), the fourth (F) and fifth (G). This first workout, to be played along to a backing track, shows you how this is mapped out, using root positions first of all.

AUDIO: Workout 1

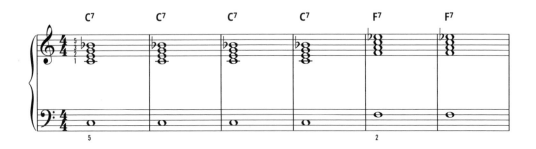

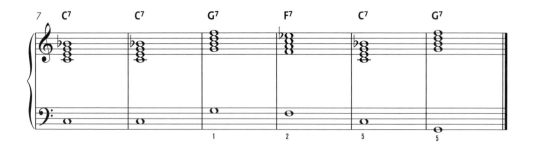

Try to memorise the left-hand part for this workout as a series of numbers. You'll be able to apply this to any basic blues progression in the future, and will serve as a good basis to understand the structure of the 12-bar blues. In our example, the final chord is the fifth: this 'helps' the sequence to repeat, but if you were playing this through just once, you could opt to end on the tonic instead.

WORKOUT 2

We can replace the root position chords with various inverted right-hand chords: hear how much more musical it sounds.

AUDIO: Workout 2

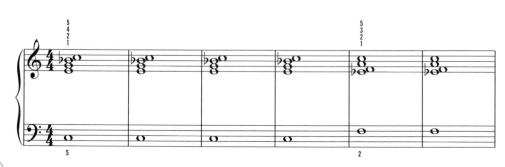

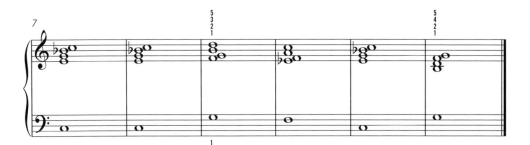

PERFORMANCE PIECE

If you are jamming with other musicians, you will rarely play a 12-bar sequence from a piece of written music, because it's a set sequence of just three chords. However, a 12 bar is only a template, and to make it sound good you need to have some ideas for rhythm and chord voicings. So this performance piece gives you a

written accompaniment for a 12-bar blues in C, which you can either play as read, or take ideas from to make up your own accompaniment.

That is also why there are no dynamic markings in this piece, as the blues is basically an improvised form – just try and put in some of your own highs and lows.

Note: to an eights feel, not swung.
AUDIO: Performance Piece
AUDIO: Performance Piece Piano

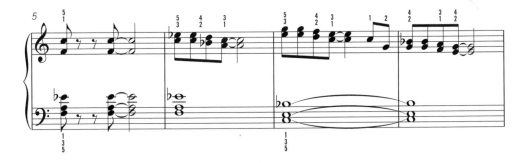

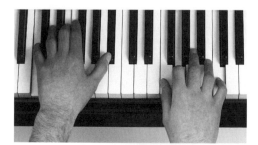

THELONIOUS MONK

*Monk, the quintessential jazz genius, created a new take on traditional blues with his eccentric performances. Check out **Blue Monk:** a pure 12-bar classic.*

GOAL: *TO PLAY A SOLO OVER A 12-BAR BLUES SEQUENCE AND TO LEARN ABOUT TRIPLETS*

This chapter gives you the chance to play a blues style solo along to the backing track on the DVD. Before we do that, we need to learn about a new rhythm – the triplet.

TRIPLETS

A triplet is a group of three notes that, in the case of simple time, lasts for a crotchet beat. Triplet rhythms are heavily used in blues – they help to give the *swung*, or 'chugging' feel that characterises many well-known blues pieces. Written out below and demonstrated on the DVD are a few bars mixed up with crotchets and triplets, so you can hear what they sound like.

AUDIO: Illustration 1

Notes to be played as part of a triplet rhythm have a '3' written above them.

Two notes can also be played within a single triplet rhythm beat. A triplet rhythm lasts the same length (one crotchet beat) if it has three notes or two, so divide the triplet beat into three, play the first note for a count of two and the second note for a count of one. This type of rhythm is commonly found in blues and once you've heard it, you won't forget it.

AUDIO: Illustration 2

WORKOUT

AUDIO: Workout

Here's an exercise to get you used to playing triplet rhythms. This follows a 12-bar chord sequence, so you can play it over the backing tracks as well.

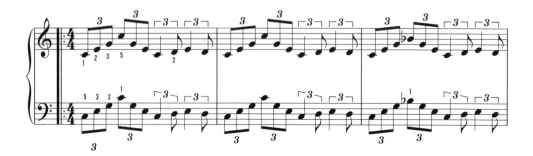

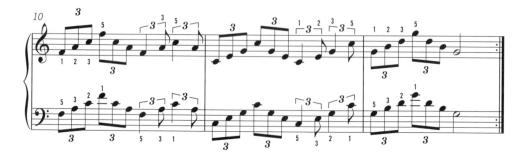

PERFORMANCE PIECE

This chapter features a piano solo over a 12-bar blues in C and is to be used along with the backing track. Over a 12-bar blues, a pianist either accompanies or solos. You had a go at accompanying in the previous chapter, so we're going to have a go at playing a (written) solo for this performance piece. An experienced blues player would normally improvise (make up) a solo over a 12-bar chord sequence, so use this written solo as a starting point to start making up your own ideas. The backing track will go round the whole 12-bar sequence once, with an instrument playing a tune (or *head*, as it is known) and then it's over to you!

AUDIO: Performance Piece

Solo over twelve bar blues in C

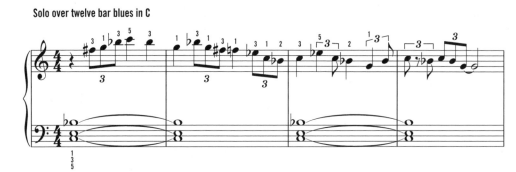

TIP

Before you try this performance piece, make sure you've gone through the blues scale from the directory at the back of the book. The solo draws heavily on the shapes and notes used in the scale.

This solo uses a lot of syncopation – accented notes off the beat, sometimes combined with tied notes. You will hear, and feel, how this anticipates the 12-bar chord movements. As in the previous chapter, there are no dynamic markings so feel free to make up your own mind.

Courtesy LFI

ELTON JOHN
The Godmother of pop has made the piano a major feature of his recordings and extravagant performances.

GOAL: TO PLAY A BASIC POP MUSIC PIANO PART, LEARNING ABOUT
VOICINGS AND DIFFERENT RIGHT-HAND/LEFT-HAND RHYTHMS

*Pop music can make slightly different
playing demands compared to Classical
styles. Usually, both hands have got well-
defined roles – the right hand will play the
main chords and maybe a tune, and the
left hand will play the notes at the bottom
of the chord, usually in a rhythm that
helps keep the track moving along. This is
known as a bass line.*

In a pop song, the piano can either accompany a solo
vocalist, a group of musicians, or it can be a featured
instrument, playing melodies.

- The Beatles and the Rolling Stones often used piano
  as an accompanying instrument, often to many of
  their best known hits. Coldplay and Keane are good
  examples of modern bands that use the piano as
  important parts of their group sound.

- Singer/songwriters such as Elton John sometimes
  used the piano less as an accompanying instrument
  and more as the main feature of a pop track, playing
  the tune either in certain sections or even all the
  way through.

WORKOUT

AUDIO: Workout

This concentrates on one of the most important things
to master in pop piano playing – hand independence.
Because the left hand often has to help to keep the
rhythm going, playing other parts with your right hand
can be trickier than you think. Play the workout slowly,
breaking down the rhythm into smaller note values to
help you get everything in the right place.

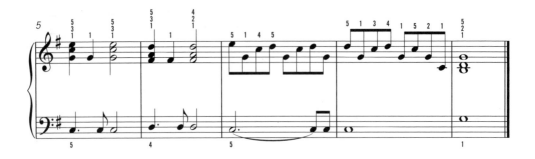

PERFORMANCE PIECE

In the style of a modern piano-driven pop song, this performance piece starts and ends by using the piano as the main feature, mixed in with more accompaniment-type passages in bars 9–10 and 13–14.

Try and feel the pulse of four running through each bar, and the way the constant repetition of this leads to the track creating a *groove*. It may take a little time to get used to the strong syncopation in the left hand, and to play both hands together.

Again, there are no dynamic markings, as this is left to the performer's individual interpretation. By listening to the backing track, you'll hear and sense the right direction.

AUDIO: Performance Piece
AUDIO: Performance Piece Piano

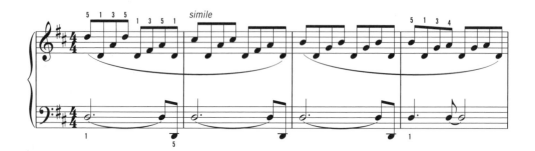

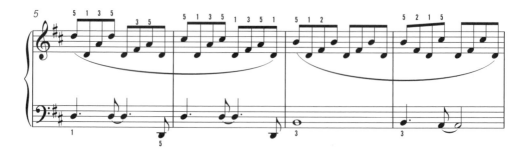

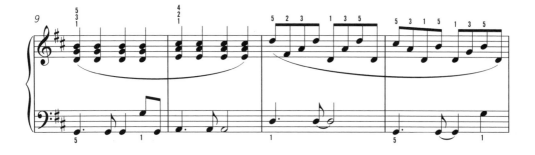

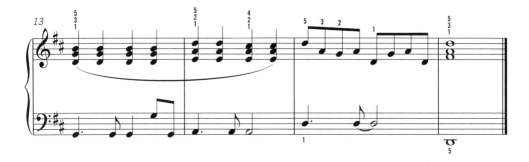

SUMMARY

There is more to good pop piano playing than you might think and a lot of it has to do with subtle syncopation. It can take a bit of work to get each hand to play different rhythms at the same time, so don't feel frustrated if it doesn't come straight away.

Remember, every new style has techniques of its own which need to be learned. By opening your mind to as many different musical genres as possible, you'll make this easier for yourself and become a better player.

GOAL: *TO PLAY AN ACCOMPANIMENT AND SOLO OVER A SHORT JAZZ PASSAGE*

WORKOUTS:
MINOR AND MAJOR NINTHS

Jazz is one of the hardest musical forms to describe. It uses a mixture of influences from across the board – from Romantic and Impressionist music, to blues, folk and boogie woogie, to name a few. The main point about playing jazz is that it is meant to be a style that breaks free from accepted forms and boundaries. There are set sequences and sets of scales that are commonly used in jazz, but these are best viewed as starting points to help get your own ideas together.

The ability to improvise – make up music as you go along – is an important part of advanced jazz accompaniment and soloing. The purpose of this short chapter is designed to get you started, show you how some basic jazz chords and rhythms are made up, and for you to play a short written accompaniment and solo along to a backing track. You can then use the backing track to improvise over to your heart's content!

JAZZ CHORDS

Jazz uses more of the dissonant harmonies that we first saw in the chapters on Impressionist music and the blues. Now we are going to encounter a couple more – major and minor ninths.

MAJOR NINTH CHORD

A major ninth uses the major seventh chord as a starting point, and then adds another note on top – a ninth above whatever the tonic note is. So to play C major 9, first of all start off with a C major 7...
AUDIO: Illustration 1

...and add a ninth on top, which is D.
AUDIO: Illustration 2

MINOR NINTH CHORD

Minor ninths use a minor seventh chord as their base, and then add a ninth on top, in exactly the same way as a major ninth chord:

AUDIO: Illustration 3

To help you get all these major and minor sevenths and ninths into some kind of order, here are those chords written down in every key from C to B.

WORKOUT 1

goes through all of the root position major, major seventh and major ninth chords.

AUDIO: Workout 1

WORKOUT 2

goes through all the root position minor, minor seventh and minor ninth chords.

AUDIO: Workout 2

Once you have got them feeling comfortable, play them in time along to the backing track.

PERFORMANCE PIECE

There are two parts to this performance piece – a *comping*, or accompanying part, and a soloing part. Both parts are set over the same chord sequence that runs all the way through the backing track, so you can practise either comping or soloing, or both.

This piece is set in one of the most recognisable styles of jazz – swing. Swing jazz can be set in a fast or slow tempo, but is almost always centred on a *walking bass line*. This is a constant, steady sequence of notes, played by the bass player, over which the other instruments in the group comp or solo.

The walking bass line is a firm rhythmical bedrock, which leaves plenty of space for the other instruments to play off-beat, syncopated rhythms.

AUDIO: Performance Piece Comping

Comping

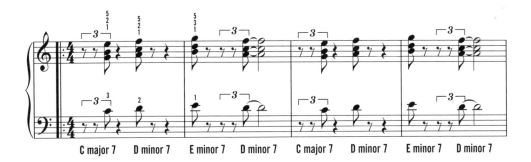

C major 7   D minor 7   E minor 7   D minor 7   C major 7   D minor 7   E minor 7   D minor 7

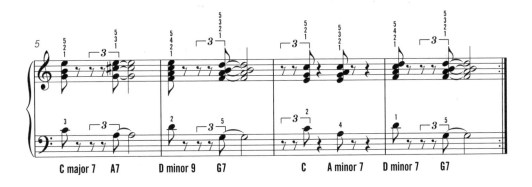

C major 7   A7   D minor 9   G7   C   A minor 7   D minor 7   G7

Solo

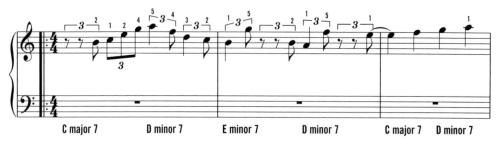

C major 7   D minor 7   E minor 7   D minor 7   C major 7   D minor 7

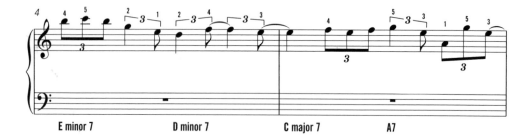

E minor 7   D minor 7   C major 7   A7

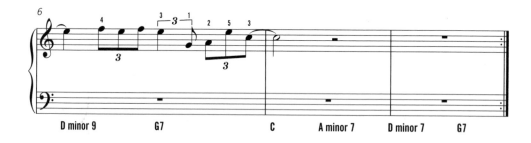

D minor 9   G7   C   A minor 7   D minor 7   G7

AUDIO: Performance Piece Solo

When playing jazz, blues or pop, there is often only a very basic part from which to read. This may be nothing more than the names of the chords written down on a piece of paper! So, when you've got comfortable with the written comping and solo parts and want to experiment, you can try putting your own versions of chords, or playing your own solo, over the chord changes written underneath each bar.

SUMMARY

The purpose of this chapter is to give you a quick experience of some of the chords and harmonies found in jazz. Studying jazz is a lifetime's work in itself, but you can learn as much from listening as anything else. Even if you want to leave

playing jazz for some time in the future, listen to as much as you can. You'll pick up ideas for phrasing, soloing and improvisation this way.

FINALLY...

We have come to the end of the last chapter, but, I hope, not to the end of your studies on the piano. You can carry on improving and learning for a lifetime, should you want to.

But, as you've discovered, there's more to playing music than just learning new techniques and styles, it's about finding that bit of you that makes music mean something. Putting passion and personality into music is what inspires and reaches out to people.

Remember that, whatever stage of ability you reach, music is a fantastic giving thing.

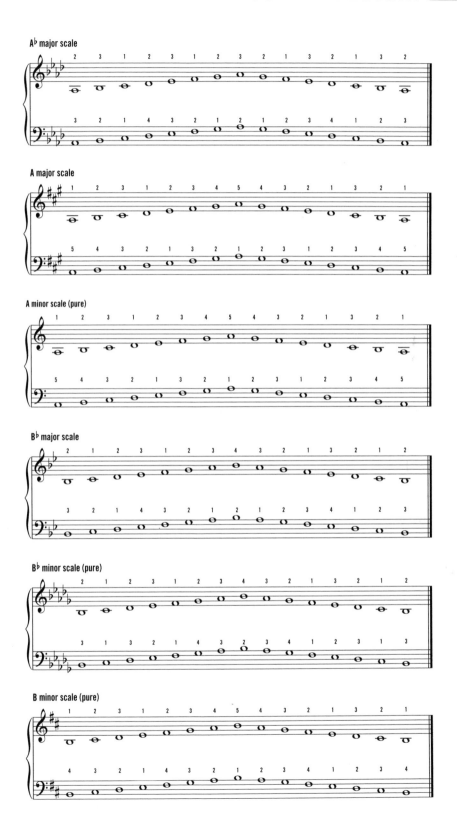

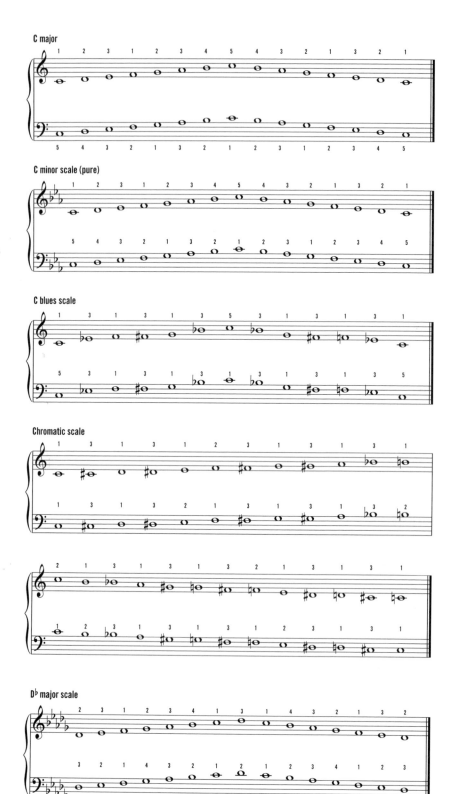

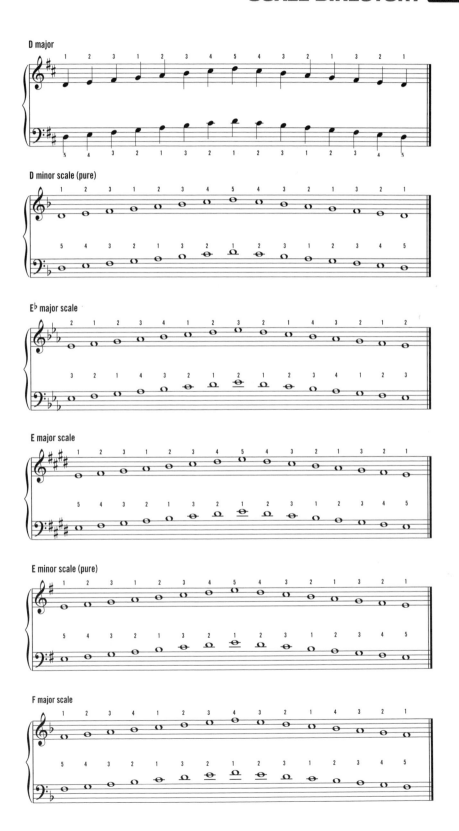

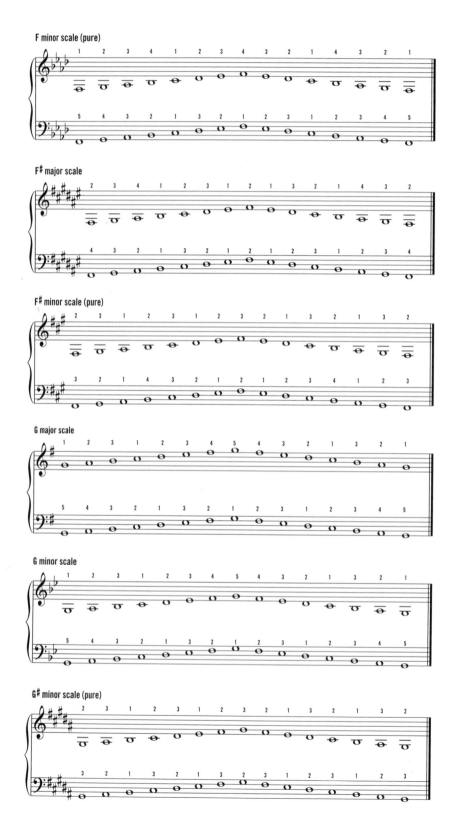

RECOMMENDED WORKS

Here is a short list of piano music from some of the composers mentioned in the book which you may enjoy playing or listening to:

J.S. Bach
Two-part inventions
Three-part inventions
French suites

Ludwig van Beethoven
Sonatinas
Solo piano sonatas

Wolfgang Amadeus Mozart
Solo piano sonatas

Frédéric Chopin
Préludes and Nocturnes

Claude Debussy
Children's Corner (piano suite)
Préludes

Paul Hindemith
Ludus Tonalis

GLOSSARY

Alberti bass: A simple arpeggiated piano accompaniment, usually played with the left hand, named after its inventor, Domenico Alberti (1710–1746)

Arpeggio: The notes of a chord played separately in succession, ascending and descending, like a scale

Bar: The way a number of beats is felt and divided in a piece of music

Barline: The point in the music dividing each group of beats

Baroque: The pre-eminent musical style between c.1600–1750

bpm: Abbreviation for *beats per minute*

Chord: A selection of at least two notes played at the same time

Classical: The pre-eminent musical style between c.1750–1800

Clef: A symbol usually placed at the start of the right-hand stave, which indicates the pitch the notes on the stave should be played at. Piano music usually uses the treble clef on the right-hand stave and the bass clef on the left-hand stave

C major scale: The major scale starting and ending on C which, uniquely, has no accidentals (sharps or flats)

Common time: Another way of describing four beats in a bar

Comping: Describes an often repetitious, accompanying part in jazz

Contrapuntal: See Counterpoint

Counterpoint: A musical style where two or more parts often imitate or overlap each other

Crotchet: A note that, in any time signature over 4 ($\frac{2}{4}$, $\frac{3}{4}$, $\frac{4}{4}$ etc) lasts for one beat

Dissonant: Describes the sound of clashing (atonal) harmonies

Dot: A sign that, when written in after a note, lengthens its duration by half as much again

Flat: When a flat sign ♭ is placed before a note it tells you to lower it by a semitone. A *flattened* note is one that has been lowered by a semitone

Groove: A repetitious rhythm that defines or compliments the main 'feel' of a pop, blues or jazz piece

Head: The name given to the set main melody in jazz and blues

Impressionist: A style of music dating from the late 19th century, often evoking specific moods or images

119

Interval: The distance between two notes

Inversion: The re-arrangement of the notes from a root position chord

Key signature: The number of sharps or flats in a key

Legato: Italian musical term meaning 'smoothly'

Leger lines: Auxiliary lines written on, above or below a note that is beyond the higher or lower limits of the stave, to indicate pitch

Major: An arrangement of notes within a scale or a chord that has a sharpened third step

Minor: An arrangement of notes within a scale or a chord that has a flattened third step

Middle C: the C note found in the middle of the keyboard, between the two pedals

Minim: A note that, in any time signature over 4 ($\frac{2}{4}$, $\frac{3}{4}$, $\frac{4}{4}$ etc) lasts for two beats

Modulate: Musical term for changing or moving into another key

Movement: An individual section within a larger work

Natural sign: When placed before a note, cancels out a previous sharp or flat symbol

Octave: Two notes with the same key letter name that are 12 semitones apart

Phrase: A musical 'sentence' or statement, often marked with a phrase line above a stave

Quaver: a note lasting for half a crotchet

Repeat bar lines: A pair of double bar lines at the start and end of a musical section, each marked with a pair of horizontal dots, indicating that the music should be repeated

Rest: A pre-determined musical gap

Romantic period: The pre-eminent musical style between c. 1820–1910

Root position: The position of a chord when its key note is at the bottom

Scale: A succession of notes in ascending (going up) or descending (going down) steps

Semibreve: A note that, in any time signature over 4 ($\frac{2}{4}$, $\frac{3}{4}$, $\frac{4}{4}$ etc) lasts for four beats

Semiquaver: A note that, in any time signature over 4 ($\frac{2}{4}$, $\frac{3}{4}$, $\frac{4}{4}$ etc) lasts for a quarter of a beat

Semitone: An interval of half a tone; one twelfth part of an octave

Sharp: When a sharp sign ♯ is placed before a note it tells you to raise it by a semitone. A sharpened note is one that has been raised by a semitone

Sonata: A musical work of several movements, for solo instrument or small ensemble

Staccato: Italian musical term meaning 'detached'

Stave: The five-line framework that music notation is written on. Piano music typically has two staves, one for the lower (left) hand and one for the upper (right) hand

Syncopation: Describes music that is accented off the beat

Tie: A joining line written between two notes that joins their two-note length values together

Time signature: A description of the amount of beats in each bar, and the length of each beat

Tone: The interval between the first two notes of the major scale

Triad: A three-note chord based around the root note, third and fifth notes of a major or minor scale

Twelve bar: A popular sequence of three chords, often found in blues and rock and roll, that is set in a 12-bar sequence

20th-century music: A musical style that evolved in the early part of the 20th century, with strong anti-Romantic elements

Two-part invention: The name given by J.S. Bach to 15 short two-part keyboard compositions

Unison: Note, or notes, at the same pitch

Walking bass line: A constant, steady sequence of notes played by a bass player, usually found in blues or jazz

08/10 (175154)